Splendors of Imperial China

Splendors of Imperial China

Treasures from the National Palace Museum, Taipei

Maxwell K. Hearn

The Metropolitan Museum of Art, New York
National Palace Museum, Taipei
Rizzoli International Publications, Inc., New York

This publication is issued in conjunction with the exhibition "Splendors of Imperial China: Treasures from the National Palace Museum, Taipei," held at The Metropolitan Museum of Art, New York, from March 19 to May 19, 1996; The Art Institute of Chicago from June 29 to August 25, 1996; the Asian Art Museum of San Francisco from October 14 to December 8, 1996; and the National Gallery of Art, Washington, D.C., from January 27 to April 6, 1997.

The exhibition has been organized by the National Palace Museum, Taipei, and The Metropolitan Museum of Art, New York.

All works in the exhibition are on loan from the National Palace Museum, Taipei.

The exhibition is made possible by Acer, Inc.

The exhibition is supported in part by The Henry Luce Foundation, Inc., the Starr Foundation, the National Endowment for the Humanities, the National Endowment for the Arts, an indemnity from the Federal Council on the Arts and the Humanities, and the Chiang Ching-Kuo Foundation. Transportation assistance has been provided by China Airlines.

Published jointly by The Metropolitan Museum of Art, New York, and the National Palace Museum, Taipei
Copyright © 1996 The Metropolitan Museum of Art, New York, and the National Palace Museum, Taipei

Distributed to the trade by Rizzoli International Publications, Inc.
300 Park Avenue South, New York, New York 10010

John P. O'Neill, Editor in Chief
Barbara Burn, Executive Editor
Tsang Seymour Design Studio, Designer
Gwen Roginsky and Chris Zichello, Production

All photographs for this volume were taken in Taipei by Bruce White.

Separations by Professional Graphics, Inc., Rockford, Illinois
Printed and bound by Arnoldo Mondadori Editore, S.p.A., Verona, Italy

Jacket/cover: Anonymous (15th century),
Portrait of the Yung-lo Emperor (plate 53)
Frontispiece: Detail of Dragon Among Flowers. Album leaf from Lou-hui chi-chin ts'e. Northern Sung dynasty (early 12th century). Silk tapestry, l. 12⅜ in. (31.3 cm), w. 8⅞ in. (22.5 cm)
Page 6: Detail, plate 9

Library of Congress Cataloging-in-Publication Data
Kuo li ku kung po wu yüan.
        Splendors of Imperial China: treasures from the National Palace Museum,
    Taipei / Maxwell K. Hearn.
            p.   cm.
        Exhibition catalog.
        ISBN 0-87099-766-1 (pbk.: alk. paper)—0-8478-1959-0 (hc.; Rizzoli)
        1. Art, Chinese—Exhibitions. 2. Art—Taiwan—Taipei—Exhibitions.
    3. Kuo li ku kung po wu yüan—Exhibitions.
    I. Hearn, Maxwell K. II. Title
    N3750.T32A66   1996
    709'.51'0747471—dc20   95-46590
                                                          CIP

Contents

Foreword

The holdings of the National Palace Museum, a repository of more than 600,000 works of art made up largely of the personal collection of the Ch'ien-lung emperor (reigned 1736–95), epitomizes China's traditional view of its own past. While there are occasional lacunae resulting from the biases of imperial taste, the palace collection still affords an unsurpassed view of Chinese civilization's evolution from its inception through the eighteenth century.

Only two major exhibitions of Chinese art from this fabled collection have been seen in the West. The first, the "International Exhibition of Chinese Art," was held in 1935–36 at the Royal Academy of Arts in London; the second, "Chinese Art Treasures," toured the United States in 1961–62 and was on view at the Metropolitan Museum for seven weeks in the fall of 1961. These two great exhibitions opened the eyes of the Western public to the artistic traditions of Chinese civilization and provided an extraordinary stimulus to the study of Chinese culture in the Western world.

In 1991, when Dr. Chin Hsiao-yi, Director of the National Palace Museum, Taipei, visited the Metropolitan, the subject of a possible loan exhibition was first broached by Dr. Wen Fong, Consultative Chairman of the Department of Asian Art. Dr. Chin responded by suggesting that the time was right to select the very best from the Palace Museum's collections to form the most comprehensive exhibition of Chinese art ever held.

Chosen by Wen Fong and James Watt, the Metropolitan's Brooke Russell Astor Senior Curator of Asian Art, and with the full cooperation of the National Palace Museum staff, the present exhibition comprises 140 masterworks of painting and calligraphy and 335 objects of jade, bronze, porcelain, and other media, including many works of art unavailable anywhere else in the world. A 664-page book entitled *Possessing the Past: Treasures from the National Palace Museum, Taipei*, presents these 475 works as a comprehensive history of Chinese art and culture divided by dynasty and medium. In this publication, *Splendors of Imperial China*, Maxwell Hearn, Curator in the Department of Asian Art at the Metropolitan and an active participant in the organization of the exhibition, has made a selection of 107 works from the exhibition, often juxtaposing different kinds of objects in order to emphasize aesthetic relationships.

This unique opportunity to display many of China's greatest artistic monuments within the pluralistic cultural environment of American museums enables us to make connections between the civilization of China and that of the West. The objects presented here certainly have an appeal that is universal, like all great art, but they also enhance our appreciation for the diversity of artistic expression and help focus attention on some of the essential qualities that make China's cultural heritage distinct from that of the West. We are particularly grateful for the unwavering support of Dr. Chin and his capable staff at the National Palace Museum for making this historic joint project possible.

Philippe de Montebello
Director, The Metropolitan Museum of Art

The Cultural Heritage

The foundations of Chinese civilization reach back five thousand years to the Neolithic and Bronze Ages. These early cultures are represented by their quintessential media: jade and bronze. Objects fashioned of these valuable materials functioned as ornaments or as implements for use in ritual practice.

Most Neolithic jades have been excavated from tomb sites. Many were made in imitation of axes, knives, and other utilitarian implements; others, such as the perforated disk (pi) and square tube (tsung), are purely abstract and geometric in form. Because these objects show no sign of use, they are believed to have played a symbolic role as offerings to gods and ancestors.

During the Bronze Age, the artistic evolution of jade and bronze artifacts corresponded to shifts in political power. In the Shang dynasty (ca. 1600–ca. 1100 B.C.), which was centered around the lower Yellow River valley of northeastern China, kings derived their authority from divine ancestors. Offerings of food and wine were made to these deities in massive bronze vessels that were either buried with a deceased clan member or used on aboveground altars. The stylized animal decoration commonly seen on these ritual vessels is thought to have served a protective role for the offerings within. Early bronzes were cast using an assemblage of sectional molds made of clay. The architectonic forms of the vessels and the arrangement of the decoration in horizontal bands are the results of this technique of manufacture.

In the eleventh century B.C., the Shang were conquered by the Chou, a people from northwestern China. The Chou claimed themselves as legitimate successors, asserting that the Shang, through misrule, had forfeited the Mandate of Heaven. During the long Chou dynasty, which lasted more than eight centuries, until 256 B.C., the ritual uses of jade and bronze were gradually supplanted by ornamental functions as these materials came to be employed in ostentatious displays of material wealth and power. Under Chou rule, the empire was divided into a number of fiefdoms that increasingly paid only token allegiance to the Chou king. As rivalries between these feudal states grew, bronze vessels became a means of manifesting political authority, as indicated by the inscriptions they bear. Whereas inscriptions on Shang bronzes typically give only the name of the ancestor to whom they are dedicated, Chou inscriptions commemorate the living by memorializing such events as military exploits, enfeoffments, treaties, and weddings. With this shift in function, the complex zoomorphic iconography of the Shang lost its significance and was replaced by an allover surface ornamentation dominated by abstract patterns of intertwined dragons.

Jade remained an important medium for ritual objects throughout the Bronze Age, but the repertoire of jade forms was greatly expanded as it also became an important material for personal adornment. During the Shang and early Chou periods, a diverse range of stylized animal and human forms were worn as auspicious amulets. By the Middle Chou period, these talismans had become elaborately worked and highly polished pieces of jewelry that proclaimed the status of the owner.

The unification of China by the First Emperor of the Ch'in dynasty in 221 B.C. ushered in an imperial era that was maintained with few interruptions until the twentieth century. While the Ch'in dynasty collapsed after only fourteen years, the ensuing Han dynasty lasted four centuries. Contemporary with the Roman empire and ruling an area of equivalent size and prosperity, the Han was an age of economic and political expansion that established many of the political patterns of later Chinese government.

With political unification, the rule of man superseded that of supernatural powers and many ancient ritual forms lost their potency. Han bronze vessels were limited to utilitarian functions and ornamentation was reduced to a minimum. Weights and measures were standardized and a uniform legal code was established. In their terse inscriptions, which simply state the container's capacity and place of manufacture, Han bronze vessels reflect the legalistic nature of the society. With the new belief in man's importance, there arose a desire to replicate magically the world of the living in the afterlife. Lifelike ceramic figures were made to accompany the deceased on their journey, and fabulous beasts, both monumental and miniature in size, began to appear in the form of three-dimensional sculptures. Jade, associated with physical and ritual purity, was identified as a medium that could preserve the body and aid the soul in its journey to the heavenly realm. Thus, burial suits of jade were made for the Han nobility, and the *pi* disk again became a potent symbol of the power of jade to purify and transform human beings into immortals.

One of the most significant outgrowths of political unification was the standardization of the written language. In spite of the continued existence of numerous spoken dialects, the written language has remained one of the defining attributes of Chinese civilization and is a key source of cultural identity. It has been from the beginning and continues to this day to be revered as an art form. The calligraphy of the Shang, Chou, and Ch'in periods is called seal script, with characters in pictographic forms of different sizes and shapes made in strokes of even thickness with a stylus or cutting instrument. In the Han period, the written language evolved into a set of standardized, rectilinear forms called clerical script. Both seal and clerical scripts are frontal and emblemlike, with balanced, architectonically built forms whose horizontal and vertical strokes cross each other at right angles. When the brush replaced the stylus as the standard writing implement in the second and third centuries, the written language rapidly evolved into its final form, called regular script. Two other, more abbreviated forms of writing, running and cursive scripts, developed about the same time, replacing the formal, rigidly frontal structure of the clerical with a casual, fluent, and relatively unstructured three-dimensionality.

Writing not only served as an instrument of imperial legitimation, appearing on state monuments and mortuary stele, and as a medium for documentation, in transcriptions of official texts, but it was also appreciated as an art form, enjoyed for its visual poetry and expressive spontaneity.

Following the collapse of the Han dynasty, China endured four centuries of political fragmentation before unity was restored under the T'ang dynasty (618–907). One of first acts of the new regime was the establishment of a new, officially sanctioned writing style, a regular script that combined attributes of earlier informal writings with the formal, monumental forms seen on stone engravings. This state-sponsored script quickly became the orthodox writing style for all official documents. With the evolution of the five basic scripts (seal, clerical, regular, running, and cursive) complete, later calligraphers were free to use these fundamental script types to explore the expressive potential of this great inherited tradition.

1. Jade disk (pi). Late Neolithic
period to Shang dynasty
(second millennium B.C.)

Jade, one of the hardest and toughest substances in nature, requires too much labor to make it practical for tools, yet the complexity of its coloration, its sheen when polished, and its musical quality when struck led the Neolithic peoples of China to prefer it for ritual objects and ornaments. This perforated disk, or pi, has no obvious practical or ornamental use and is thought to have served a ritual or symbolic function. It dates to the late Neolithic period, when jade pi were often laid on top of the body in burials. In historic times, because of its round shape, the pi was regarded as symbolic of heaven; it was also valued as a token of wealth and political legitimacy. This ancient example was inscribed in the Ch'ing dynasty by the Ch'ien-lung emperor (reigned 1736–95).

Bronze, like jade, was emblematic of wealth and power. In their sacrificial offerings to the gods and royal ancestors from whom they derived their authority to rule, the kings of the Shang dynasty used ritual vessels cast in bronze. The forms of these vessels often derived from earlier models; the prototype of this bronze ting tripod, for example, was a ceramic cooking pot. Its grand size, the lavish use of precious metal, the powerful animal iconography, and the inscription all serve to transform what had originally been a utilitarian object into a work of imposing ritual significance.

2. Bronze tripod vessel (ting).
Late Shang dynasty (13th–mid-
11th century B.C.)

4. Pair of jade pendants (p'ei).
Warring States period
(481–221 B.C.)

3. Bronze wine vessel (hu).
Late Western Chou dynasty
(mid-9th century–771 B.C.)

The ritual use of jade and bronze was superseded by their use as ornament. During the Chou dynasty, they became ostentatious signs of material wealth and power. The intricate patterns and animal-mask motifs of the Shang dynasty (pl. 2) have been simplified in this bronze wine vessel into a bold interlace of symmetrically intertwined serpents whose function is now more decorative than protective. The similarly shaped jade dragons originally served as part of a pendant that would have hung from the belt of an aristocrat. Between the dragons a bead was suspended as a clapper, so that when its wearer moved about, the pendant acted as a chime, drawing attention to the proud owner. The overall pattern of knobby curls that covers the surface was created through a laborious process in which the ground was polished away. It demanded a degree of technical virtuosity that was not surpassed until two thousand years later, in the eighteenth century.

5. Bronze standard measure
(*liang*). Wang Mang
Interregnum, dated A.D. 9

With the political unification of China under the Ch'in
(221–206 B.C.) and Han (206 B.C.–A.D. 220) dynasties, the rule
of man superseded the influence of supernatural powers and
ancient ritual forms lost their potency. Weights and measures
were standardized throughout the empire and bronze vessels,
given regularized shapes and sizes, were reduced to a utilitarian
function, a transformation exemplified in this *liang*, a standard
measure. Shorn of all ritual and decorative embellishment, the
vessel has only a long inscription that proclaims a new set of
volumetric standards that this vessel and its attached measuring
cups were intended to enforce. Together with the notion of
man's enhanced significance within the cosmos came a new
interest in the pursuit of immortality. The jade chimera exemplifies the kind of fabulous beasts that were envisioned during
the later Han dynasty either as tomb guardians or as vehicles
for transporting their human charges into the afterlife.

6. Jade chimera (*pi-hsieh*). Han
dynasty (206 B.C.–A.D. 220)

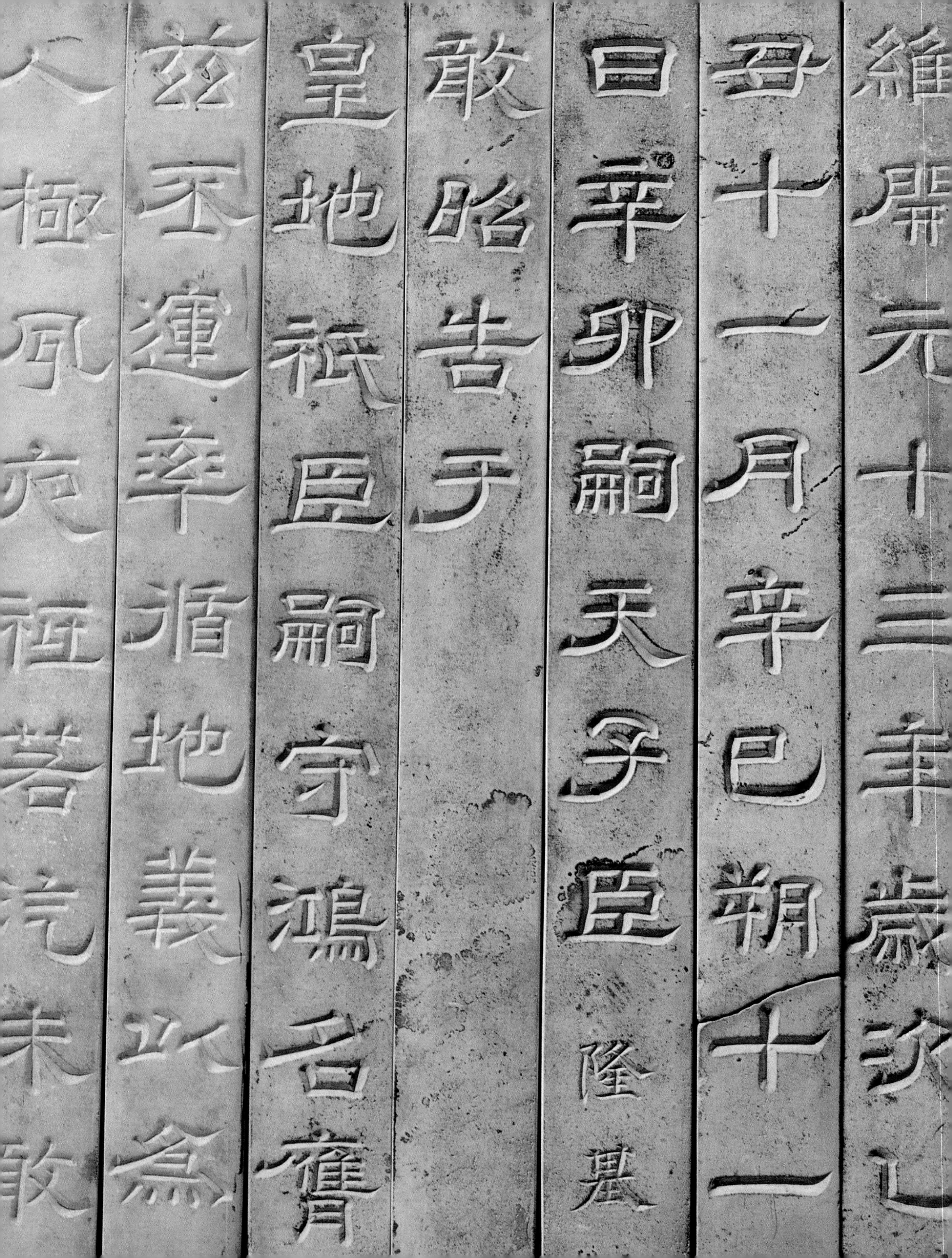
維開元十三年歲次乙
丑十一月辛巳朔十一
日辛卯嗣天子臣隆基
敢昭告于
皇地祇臣嗣守鴻名膺
茲丕運率循地義以為
人極夙夜祗若汔未敢

Institutional power was often conveyed in China through monumental inscriptions cast in bronze or carved in stone. In the year 725, the T'ang emperor Hsüan-tsung journeyed to Mount T'ai to make sacrificial offerings to the deities of heaven and earth, an event of great significance in his reign. The ritual text was recorded and displayed on these marble tablets, which were then buried at the altar site. Not only the content but the style of the writing, carved in the monumental clerical style of the earlier Han period (206 B.C.–A.D. 220), served as confirmation of Hsüan-tsung's legitimacy as the ruler of a great empire. As the role of the individual grew in Chinese society, greater value was placed on unique interpretations of the written language, particularly in personal letters, the most private form of communication. The fourth-century calligrapher Wang Hsi-chih, revered as the patriarch of brush writing, was noted for his mastery of running script, the informal writing style most often used in personal correspondence. In the example at the right, the rigid frontality characteristic of the archaic clerical script has been superseded by a fluent three-dimensionality, with Wang's flicking, turning brushwork suggesting rapid movement in space.

7. Bound marble tablets, dated 725 (detail)

8. Early T'ang tracing copy of Wang Hsi-chih (303–361). Handscroll: *Three Passages of Calligraphy: P'ing-an, Ho-ju, and Feng-chü* (detail)

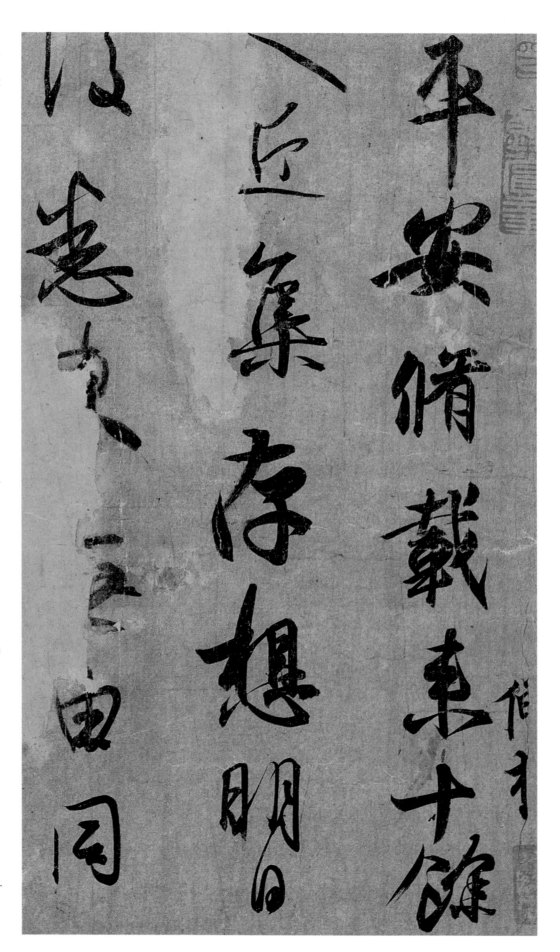

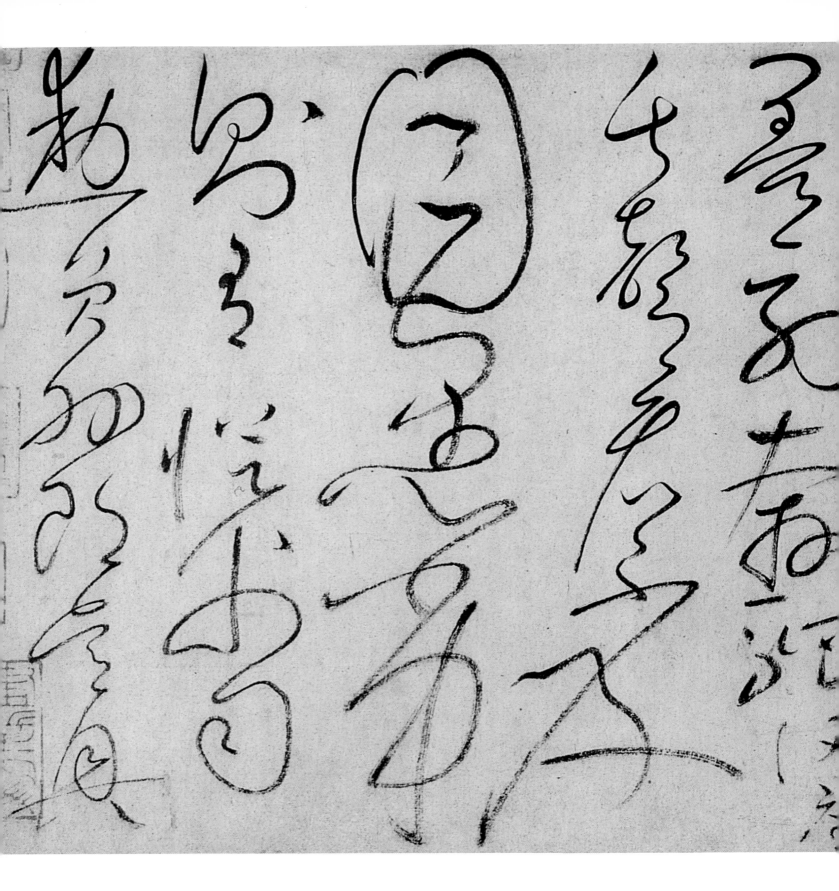

9. Huai-su (ca. 735–ca. 799).
Handscroll: *Autobiographical
Essay*, dated 777 (detail)

The *Autobiographical Essay* is the quintessence of writing as spontaneous expression, both of the human spirit and of the forms
and movement of nature. Huai-su, the eighth-century Buddhist
monk who wrote this piece, was a practitioner of Ch'an (Zen,
in Japanese) Buddhism, a sect that encouraged spontaneity and
individualism in the pursuit of enlightenment rather than an
adherence to set rules or dogmas. Huai-su demonstrated his

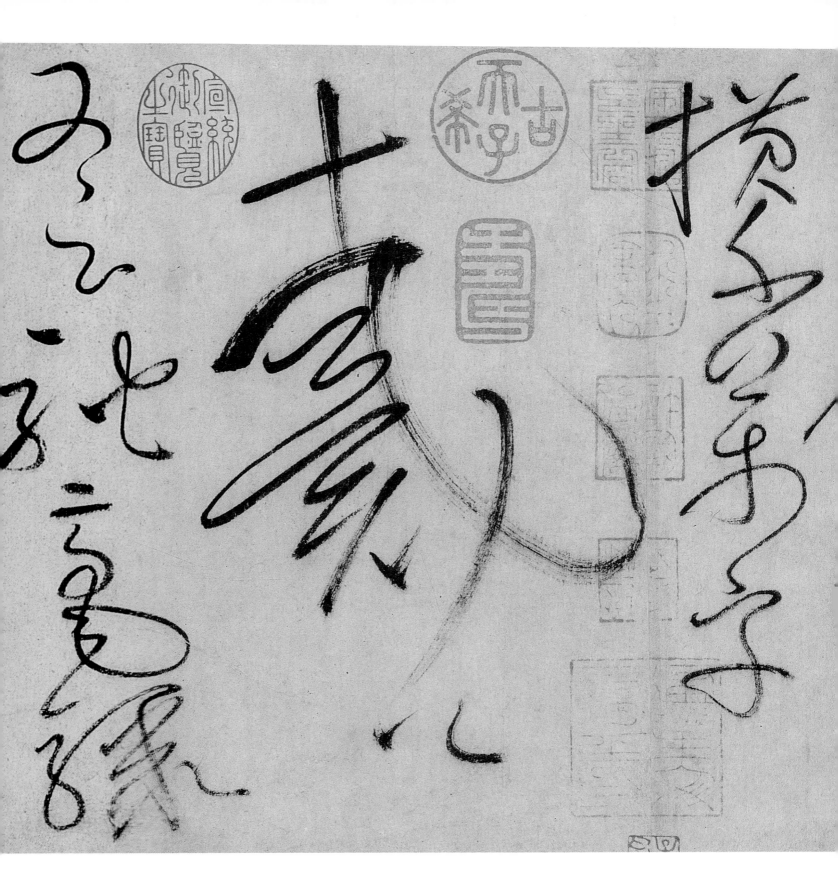

own unorthodox nature through his fluid cursive style. According to his contemporaries, Huai-su did his best work while inebriated, when, in a state of high exhilaration, "his mind and his hand, in the pursuit of pure adventure, worked together in perfect harmony." In this example, the characters, rooted in the cursive tradition of Wang Hsi-chih (see pl. 8), vary dramatically in size and shape and are linked in an unin-terrupted flow of darting, looped brushstrokes. With his brush coursing over the paper with explosive speed, Huai-su transforms the wild cursive into a force of nature. "Good calligraphy," he once remarked, "is like a flock of birds darting out from trees, a startled snake scurrying into the grass, or cracks bursting through a shattered wall."

21

The Sung Dynasty: A New Cultural Universe

The Sung dynasty (960–1279) was culturally the most brilliant era in later imperial China. A time of great social and economic change, the Sung period in large measure shaped the intellectual and political climate of China down to the twentieth century. The first half of the dynasty, when the capital was located in the north, at Pien-ching (modern K'ai-feng), Honan Province, is known as the Northern Sung (960–1127). In 1127 Pien-ching was sacked and northern China was occupied by the Jurchen, a nomadic people from the far north. The Jurchen established their own Chin dynasty (1115–1234), and the remnants of the Sung court fled to south of the Yangtze River. The Chinese capital was eventually reestablished at Hangchow, and from there a reduced empire was governed for another one hundred fifty years. This latter period is known as the Southern Sung (1127–1279).

In contrast to the preceding T'ang dynasty, which ruled through the delegation of power to aristocratic families, often of military descent, the first Sung emperor, T'ai-tsu (reigned 960–76), succeeded in reducing the power of the military by promoting a centralized bureaucracy staffed entirely by civil officials. While the displacement of the old aristocracy contributed to a greater concentration of power in the office of the emperor, the recruitment of civil bureaucrats through a national examination system led to the rise of a meritocracy of scholar-officials that owed its authority not to aristocratic birthright but to scholarly achievement. Under the Sung, with enhanced social mobility, a rapid expansion of commerce and urban life, technological advances, and growth in productivity, the empire flourished and an era of peace and prosperity was ushered in.

The first part of the Sung dynasty witnessed the flowering of one of the supreme artistic expressions of Chinese civilization: monumental landscape painting. During the period of social and political chaos that accompanied the fall of the T'ang dynasty in 907, scholars retreated to the mountains, living in hermitages or in Buddhist temples. In nature they discovered the moral order they had found lacking in the human world. The depiction of landscape—a projection onto a surface of the orderly world of nature— became the expression of their faith in man's harmonious existence in the universe.

Monumental depictions of landscape continued to dominate painting throughout the Northern Sung, but not without undergoing significant changes in imagery and style. By the late eleventh and early twelfth centuries, with the failure of the government's campaign for economic and political reform, the Northern Sung empire was in upheaval. Rather than expressing an affirmation of the immutability of nature, as in the tenth century, the romantic landscapes of the eleventh century reflect a world in turmoil and transition. In the early twelfth century, under Emperor Hui-tsung (reigned 1101–25), a new court-sponsored style, more harmonious and restrained, began to replace the sense of vastness characteristic of earlier Northern Sung painting. This more focused and realistic view of nature prefigures the intimate landscapes of the Southern Sung.

Painting in the Sung court came under the auspices of the Imperial Painting Academy. At the beginning of the Sung dynasty, painters from all parts of the empire were recruited by the new government to serve the needs of the court. Over time, the varied traditions represented by this group of artists were welded together into a compatible Sung academic manner, the culmination of centuries of achievement in mastering a naturalistic, closely descriptive, and convincing portrayal of the physical world. Under Emperor Hui-tsung, himself an accomplished painter and calligrapher, imperial patronage and the ruler's direct involvement in establishing artistic direction reached a zenith that would be emulated by all subsequent imperial academies. In addition to landscape, Hui-tsung's academicians specialized in religious figures, historical narratives, genre painting, flowers, birds, and animals, all keenly observed and meticulously rendered.

The momentous shift during the early Sung—from a society ruled by a hereditary aristocratic order to a society governed by a central bureaucracy of scholar-officials—also had a major impact on the arts. Sung scholar-officials quickly laid claim to calligraphy and poetry as expressive vehicles uniquely suited to their class. Dissatisfied with the rigidity and oversophistication of early Northern Sung calligraphy, eleventh-century scholars sought to revive the natural and spontaneous qualities of calligraphy of earlier centuries.

The literati also applied their new critical standards to painting. Rejecting the highly realistic descriptive style followed by the professional painters of the Imperial Painting Academy, they also departed from the official view that art must serve the state. Instead, the amateur scholar-artists pursued painting and calligraphy for their own amusement as a form of personal expression.

The stylistic direction and high technical standards established by Emperor Hui-tsung in the early twelfth century continued into the Southern Sung period (1127–1279), during which they were perpetuated through the rigorous training of the imperial workshops or through family ateliers. Southern Sung society was characterized by the pursuit of a highly aestheticized way of life, and paintings of the period often focus on evanescent pleasures and the transience of beauty. Images evoke poetic ideas that appeal to the senses or capture the fleeting qualities of a moment in time. One particularly important source of inspiration for Southern Sung artists was the natural beauty of Hangchow and its environs, particularly the West Lake, a famed scenic spot ringed with lush mountains and dotted with palaces, private gardens, and Buddhist temples.

The decorative arts also reached the height of elegance and technical perfection during the Sung. Like painting, the plastic arts responded to two different aesthetics—that of the imperial court and that of popular culture. Bronze vessels used in state rituals, ceramics and lacquers made for use in the palace, and official garments all followed conservative traditions and were based on archaic models. But luxury items produced for a broader commercial market also show an extraordinary combination of artistry and craftsmanship.

At the beginning of the Sung dynasty, ritual objects created for the court were reconstructed on the basis of often vague documentation and classical texts. During the eleventh century, however, scholars increasingly based their study of the past on actual objects. Antiquarians began avidly collecting bronzes, jades, and other archaeologically recovered objects, which became, in turn, models for more accurate court reproductions.

Supreme among the decorative arts of the Sung period are ceramics, which many connoisseurs consider the highest artistic achievement of the Chinese potter. As in painting, Sung ceramics represent the culmination of centuries of artistic experimentation and technical development. Utilitarian wares were gradually transformed into refined works of art, objects that embody the aesthetic sensibility of the age. The finest Sung ceramics, named for the kiln sites where they were produced, are characterized by simple, elegant shapes and superb glazes that seamlessly merge into an organic whole. Pottery forms perfectly exploit the properties of clay as it is thrown on a wheel, exhibiting a softness of contour and a simplicity of structure that allow the viewer to concentrate on the beauty of the glaze. Sung glazes are mostly monochromatic and usually exhibit a soft sheen and lustrous translucency without the glassy hardness of later porcelains. Often the potter would intentionally exploit the accidental effects of a glaze, allowing it to flow into thick "tears" or to develop a crackle pattern.

The religious arts also flourished during the Sung dynasty. As Confucianism, Taoism, and Buddhism—reconciled in the Unity of the Three Teachings—became an integral part of the Sung cultural milieu, learned Buddhist monks and Confucian scholar-officials interacted freely, and colorful religious pageants and richly appointed temples had a significant impact on popular culture. One regional center of Buddhism, the Ta-li kingdom, situated in what is now Yunnan Province, served as an important conduit of religious influences originating in Tibet and western Asia. The influence of non-Chinese religious doctrines and icons became particularly important after the incorporation of Ta-li into the Chinese empire during the ensuing Mongol era.

10. Anonymous (2d half of 10th
century). Hanging scroll: *Portrait
of Sung T'ai-tsu*

26

The portrait of the emperor T'ai-tsu (reigned 960–76; pl. 10), founder of the Sung dynasty, combines careful observation with deliberate idealization, creating an imposing image of the ruler as Son of Heaven. Draped in a voluminous white robe and wearing the imperial cap, its extended flaps stiffened with lacquer, T'ai-tsu is a mountain of a man, a monumental presence that conveys the strength and stability of his rule. The portrait of T'ai-tsu's great-grandson, Jen-tsung, reveals a startling shift in emphasis. A heightened concern for realism, including the meticulous reproduction of textile patterns and the carved decor of the throne, has left the image of the emperor diminished. Rather than emphasizing Jen-tsung's power and majesty, the portrait points up his sensitive and modest character, which seems all but overwhelmed by the ornate trappings of his imperial regalia.

11. Anonymous (11th century). Hanging scroll: *Portrait of Sung Jen-tsung*

Fan K'uan's majestic mountain landscape, nearly seven feet high, presents a vision of hierarchical cosmic order. Painted at the beginning of the Sung dynasty (960–1279), when society was just recovering from the chaos of dynastic collapse, Fan's image reflects a profound belief in the capacity of nature to serve as the model for human society. Like an enthroned emperor surrounded by his ministers of state, court officials, and myriad subjects, the towering central peak presides over a carefully ordered landscape. To convey the vast size of the mountain, Fan K'uan uses a leaping scale that progresses in three degrees of magnitude, from the tiny foreground figures of the mule train to the enormous middle ground trees to the towering rock face of the distant mountain, which dwarfs everything around it. The mountain's scale appears infinite because it is unmeasurable; blank intervals of space between foreground, middle distance, and background serve as significant pauses between shifting views. Fan complements this illusion of immeasurable space with an intricately detailed description of rock surfaces, foliage, and figures imbuing his landscape with a sense of eternal truth.

12. Fan K'uan (d. after 1023). Hanging scroll: *Travelers Amid Streams and Mountains*

Detail, plate 12

This image of deer in an autumn forest, though stylized and decorative, reflects the nomadic heritage of the Khitan Liao people, who once lived along China's northern borders. Although largely assimilated into Chinese society by the tenth century, the Khitan continued to assert their nomadic traditions in the arts, depicting hunting scenes of deer in autumn and wild geese and swans in spring. Where the Khitan image is timeless and idealized, another painting of animals, made a century later by the Chinese artist Ts'ui Po, focuses on the reality of the moment. Appealing to the senses, the darkened sky and bare earth proclaim the winter season. A cold wind bends the bamboo and rustles the dry oak leaves. A startled hare is immobilized by the piercing cry of a magpie. The artist makes his own presence known by a prominent display of both signature and date and through the use of bold brushstrokes—a technique that places in relief the meticulous description of the hare's soft fur.

13. Anonymous (10th–early 11th century). Hanging scroll: *Deer Among Red Maples* (detail)

14. Ts'ui Po (active ca. 1060–85). Hanging scroll: *Magpies and Hare*, dated 1061

The image of nature presented by the Northern Sung master Kuo Hsi, in contrast to the timeless, fixed world envisioned by Fan K'uan (pl. 12), is one of continuous motion, a cosmos of change and becoming. The writhing forms of the mountain, built up of layers of pale wash and dark ink contours, create an impression of mass at once emerging from and receding back into enveloping veils of mist. Views into deep space alternate with impenetrable rock walls that block the viewer's line of sight, enhancing the sense of oscillation and movement. In an image that recalls the mystical mountains of the immortals, Kuo rejects a landscape that is objectively true to nature, embracing one imbued with human emotion.

15. Kuo Hsi (1000–ca. 1090). Hanging scroll: *Early Spring*, dated 1072

Detail, plate 15

In the late eleventh century, for the first time, the practice of calligraphy and the practice of painting became one. In Wen T'ung's image of a stalk of bamboo, the artist, like the calligrapher, creates his forms by the use of conventional brushstrokes. The image is based on an objective study of nature, but its vitality derives from the artist's empathy for his subject rather than from any specific model. In the same way, the calligraphy of Wen T'ung's friend the poet Su Shih does not slavishly imitate an earlier calligraphic paradigm but represents the artist's spontaneous response both to traditional forms and to his own feelings. As the characters interact with one another, the sense of diversity among individual forms is subordinated to an overall feeling of harmony and unity, while the thick charcoal-black ink and velvety paper give Su's calligraphy a rich sensuality not seen before. Inspired by the Ch'an Buddhist notion of intuitive understanding, Su and Wen believed that spontaneity and the possibility of sudden insight were the ultimate goals of the artist. From this time forward, painting and calligraphy would become equivalent vehicles for self-expression.

16. Wen T'ung (1018–1079). Hanging scroll: *Bamboo*, ca. 1070

17. Su Shih (1037–1101). Handscroll: *Poems Written at Huang-chou on the Cold-Food Festival*, datable to 1082 (detail)

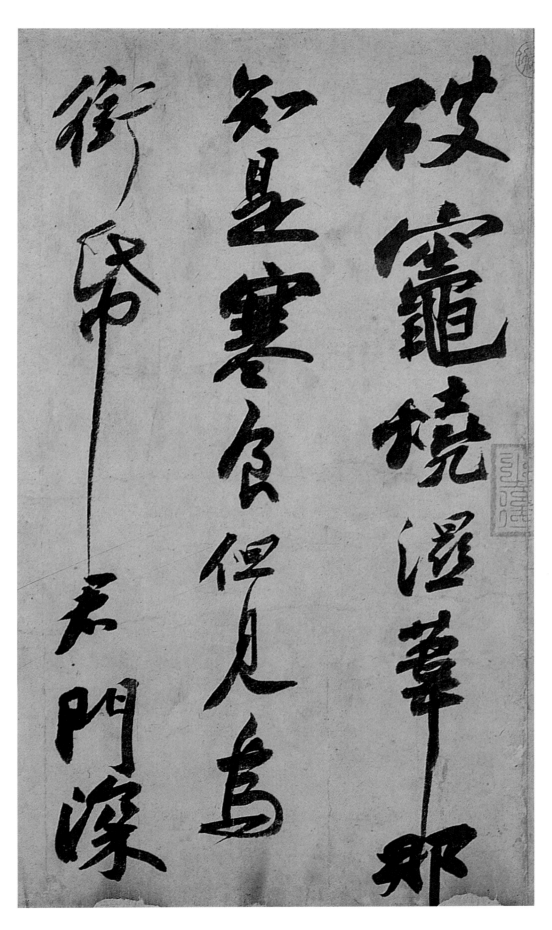

公楊少師即李西
臺筆意減使僕
漬為之東法減為此

19. Porcelain dish. Chün
ware. Sung to Yüan dynasty
(12th–13th century)

18. Huang T'ing-chien
(1045–1105). Colophon to
Su Shih's *Poems Written at Huang-
chou on the Cold-Food Festival*,
datable to 1100 (detail)

A protégé of Su Shih, Huang T'ing-chien sought to recapture
the spontaneous, informal quality seen in the calligraphy of the
fourth century (pl. 8). In this inscription or colophon written
on the blank paper following Su's *Poems Written at Huang-chou on
the Cold-Food Festival* (pl. 17), Huang reverses T'ang dynasty principles of symmetry, order, and parallel structure and stresses
asymmetry, irregularity, and oblique angles. Brushstrokes twist
and turn, and characters invade one another's space, linking
and interconnecting in a lyrical three-dimensional composition. The Chün-ware dish shows a similar appreciation for
dynamic abstract pattern; the rich purple glaze is boldly
splashed onto an opalescent blue glaze ground. Chün ware has
one of the most complex of all Chinese glazes. Potters might
induce differences in color and shading by varying the copper
content of the glaze, but they could never be entirely sure of
the outcome. Revealing an aesthetic very near to that of Huang
and other eleventh-century scholar-calligraphers, the very
spontaneity and naturalness of these accidental effects were
most valued.

20. Emperor Hui-tsung
(1082–1135; reigned
1101–25). Handscroll: *Two
Poems* (detail)

By the early twelfth century, the expressive, subjective manner
of painting and calligraphy first created by Wen T'ung (pl. 16)
and Su Shih (pl. 17) in reaction to academic, court-sanctioned
styles had itself been accepted at court and was an important
influence on imperial taste. Emperor Hui-tsung, an accomplished painter and calligrapher, carried the highly individualis-
tic approach to an extreme. His style shows refinement and
elegance, qualities that characterize his taste in all the arts. The
attenuated style of his calligraphy, known as slender gold, is
remarkable for its control and discipline; his characters, con-
structed of tautly executed strokes, appear engraved in stone
rather than brushed onto an absorbent surface. The same attention to form and proportion is also apparent in the graceful
simplicity of this Ju-ware dish. Ju ware, the supreme expression of the art of the Chinese potter, is characterized by its soft,
opalescent bluish green glaze and utterly simple forms, which
have a quality of organic naturalism. Supplied almost exclusive-
ly to the imperial palace during Hui-tsung's reign, it is today
the rarest of all Chinese wares. Fewer than one hundred pieces
have survived aboveground; the largest group and finest speci-
mens are preserved in the National Palace Museum.

化筆難月
留功獨造下青

21. Porcelain dish. Ju ware.
Northern Sung dynasty
(12th century)

23. Porcelain censer. Ting ware. Northern Sung dynasty (960–1127)

22. Porcelain long-necked bottle. Ting ware. Northern Sung dynasty (960–1127)

Sung ceramics draw inspiration from a number of sources, including ancient bronze ritual vessels, silverwork bowls and cups from the T'ang dynasty, and imported trade goods. The white-glazed Ting wares of the Northern Sung dynasty are noteworthy for the diversity of their forms. The incense burner, for example, has the same shape as a ninth-century-B.C. ritual food vessel known as a *kuei*, while the long-necked bottle appears to be modeled on a type of imported glass. Other ceramic shapes appear to be without reference to forms created first in other media, reflecting the natural behavior of clay shaped on a potter's wheel. The organic, gently swelling body of the *mei-p'ing* bottle with incised lotus designs epitomizes the potter's instinctive response to his medium.

24. Porcelain vase (*mei-p'ing*). Ting ware. Northern Sung dynasty (960–1127)

26. Silk tapestry album leaf: *Immortals in a Mountain Pavilion*. Northern Sung dynasty (early 12th century)

The revival of earlier styles influenced both painting and textiles. Li T'ang, the premier landscapist of the Imperial Painting Academy in the early twelfth century, drew inspiration from Fan K'uan (pl. 12) and other tenth-century painters in this monumental image of a towering peak and a dense grove of pines. In Li's interpretation individual motifs have been enlarged and pulled closer to the viewer; vast spaces have been compressed and the sense of grandeur relinquished for a more closely focused realism. Li's emphatic ax-cut texture strokes, while intended to recall the finely stippled granite surfaces of tenth-century pictures, are greatly enlarged here and take on a new prominence. Similarly, the design of a tapestry made at about the same time is done in a stylized, archaic manner, the dreamlike vision of paradise harking back to a golden age. The scene, which may have been inspired by a painting by Emperor Hui-tsung himself, is crowded with auspicious Taoist motifs. Aristocratic figures converse at a banquet, with a magical landscape of peach trees, flowering plants, and frolicking monkeys before them and a sky above filled with multicolored clouds and cranes.

25. Li T'ang (ca. 1070s–ca. 1150s). Hanging scroll: *Wind in the Pines Amid Ten Thousand Valleys*, dated 1124 (detail)

43

27. Porcelain bowl. Ju ware.
Northern Sung dynasty (12th
century)

The focus of much of the art produced by the Imperial
Painting Academy during the 152 years of the Southern Sung
period (1127–1279) shifted from monumental landscape to
intimate scenes of daily life in the gardens and palaces situated
near Hangchow's scenic West Lake. A favorite format for such
paintings was the circular fan, in which a painted image on
one side would be paired with a poem—often by an imperial
hand—on the other. Such a fan might serve as a small but elegant gift to a member of the court or to some deserving subject. Feng Ta-yu's glimpse of life on a lotus pond, which
features a pair of mandarin ducks, a symbol of marital harmony, is an early example of this genre. Ceramic forms too were
inspired by natural shapes. The elegant, lobed body and scal-
loped edges of this Ju-ware bowl were undoubtedly influenced
by the shape of a lotus blossom, although a closer source was
probably a similarly shaped silver vessel of the tenth century.
Such blossom-shaped bowls would originally have held a wine
pitcher, whose ambrosial contents were hinted at by the vessel's
floral form.

28. Attributed to Feng Ta-yu
(active mid-12th century).
Fan mounted as album leaf:
Lotus Pond

29. Porcelain pillow. Ting ware. Sung dynasty (960–1279)

30. Attributed to Su Han-ch'en (active ca. 1130s–60s). Hanging scroll: *Winter Play* (detail)

In the protected world of the palace garden two children play with a pet kitten beneath a blossoming plum, harbinger of spring. Originally part of a set of hanging scrolls that probably showed children in each of the four seasons, the painting is attributed to the preeminent painter of children at the Southern Sung court, Su Han-ch'en. The artist's carefully observed portrayal of a young girl and her slightly younger playmate is an indication that children of both sexes were prized in the imperial world of privilege and plenty. For most Chinese, however, concern for the continuation of the family line meant that sons were preferred to daughters. As a result, many objects relating to marriage and family life were embellished with images of little boys, including the ceramic pillow above, which was made in the hope that its user would give birth to a son.

31. Anonymous (12th century).
Hanging scroll: *Hen and Chicks*

48

The description of nature in painting was never as highly focused in China as in the twelfth century. As part of the Sung fascination with the intimate details of natural life, no creature was too insignificant for the artist's close observation and appreciation. Li Ti's portrayal of a kitten and the anonymous depiction of a hen and her chicks are tours de force in the genre known as feathers and fur. Through such vividly accurate and immediate portrayals, the artist provided fresh insights into the familiar, enabling us to empathize with his subject. At times, these seemingly casual depictions would carry a didactic message. A poem by the Ming emperor Hsien-tsung (reigned 1465–87), for example, mounted above the image of the hen and chicks, compares the virtues of the mother hen, scratching for food all the long day to feed her offspring, to the tireless benevolence of the emperor toward his subjects.

32. Li Ti (active ca. 1163– after 1197). Album leaf: *Kitten,* dated 1174

迎風呈巧媚
浥露逞紅妍

33. Ma Yüan (active
ca. 1160–after 1225). Fan
mounted as album leaf:
Apricot Blossoms

50

The single branch of blossoming apricot, by the Southern Sung academic painter Ma Yüan, exemplifies the "broken branch" convention, focusing on a corner of nature rather than on a broader landscape scene. As a gardener might arrange nature to create the setting for a flower arrangement, Ma carefully considers the placement of the branch within the frame of the album leaf. Balancing the image of the branch, a couplet in the upper right corner, added by Ma's patron, Empress Yang Mei-tzu, reads: "Meeting the wind, they offer their artful charm; moist with dew, they boast their pink beauty." Reaching out toward the inscription, the branch dramatically separates to create a perfect setting for the fine, delicate writing. Ma Yüan, though he painted this branch from his imagination, may well have admired a similar composition, delicate pink blossoms on an elegant branch of black, poised in a vase with a jadelike celadon glaze—like this one, produced about the same time at Lung-ch'üan, not far from Hangchow, the Southern Sung capital. The vase's rich, lustrous glaze, achieved through multiple glazing, illustrates why Lung-ch'üan ware became during the thirteenth and early fourteenth centuries one of the most popular ceramics in China and abroad.

34. Porcelain vase. Lung-ch'üan ware. Southern Sung dynasty (1127–1279)

35. Hsia Kuei (active
ca. 1200–ca. 1240). Handscroll:
Streams and Mountains, Pure and Remote
(detail)

Through a dazzling combination of concise brushwork and graded ink washes, Hsia Kuei creates the illusion of continuous recession into deep space seen through layers of light-suffused mist, inviting the viewer to enter the world of Sung monumental landscape. Exploiting the dramatic potential of the hand-scroll format, Hsia has composed his landscape of nearly thirty feet in interlocking segments that unfold like orchestrated movements in a symphony. As the scroll unrolls from right to left, a startling vertical cliff erupts from a wide expanse of water, described by the blank surface of the paper—the absence of painted image—and punctuated only by three boats. At the base of the cliff, two scholars attended by a servant stroll toward a pavilion to admire the view, while in the mountains two recluses converse or meditate in a cave. As the landscape grows in complexity, thrusting rock promontories emerge from the distance, only to dissolve into ghostly shadows.

Aesthetic refinement reached its zenith in thirteenth-century Sung China, particularly in the bittersweet contemplation of life's fleeting pleasures. The elite engaged in such pastimes as matching poems with paintings, tasting tea, and playing the zither (*ch'in*). One of the favorite activities of this society was the cultivation and appreciation of flowering plum trees, whose fragile blossoms and delicate perfume lasted only a few short days. In Ma Lin's painting a gentleman prepares to enjoy the flowers in one of the twenty-four prescribed ways, here by candle-light beneath a full moon. Refinement also characterizes the color, shape, and glaze of Southern Sung ceramics. Rejecting technical perfection in favor of spontaneity and naturalism, the potter who made this gourd-shaped vase intentionally induced as decoration a random pattern of cracks known as crazing, which occurs in the kiln when the glaze, as it cools, contracts at a faster rate than does the body.

36. Porcelain vase. Kuan ware. Southern Sung dynasty (1127–1279)

37. Ma Lin (ca. 1180–after
1256). Fan mounted as album
leaf: *Waiting for Guests by Candlelight*

禹

克勤于邦　烝民乃粒

懋數在躬　廟中允執

惡酒好言　九功由立

不伐不矜　振古莫及

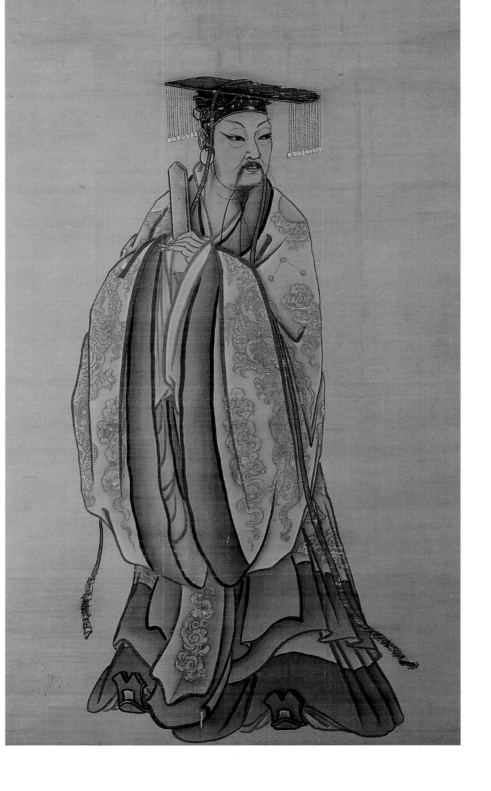

Shortly after his accession to the throne through a palace coup, Emperor Li-tsung (1205–1264; reigned 1225–64) summoned his leading court painter, Ma Lin, to paint a series of portraits depicting ancient sovereigns and Confucian sages. To these large and impressive hanging scrolls Li-tsung himself added poetic tributes. By including emperor-kings in a lineage of both philosophers and mythical rulers, the portraits illustrate the orthodox succession as transcending dynastic divisions, thus claiming merit rather than birthright as the ultimate criterion for political legitimacy. In Ma Lin's depiction of King Yü, the legendary founder of the Hsia dynasty of three thousand years earlier, the ruler is shown holding a jade tablet, symbol of his authority. The origin and early significance of such tablets remain unclear, but a similar example, datable to about 2000 B.C. on the basis of the heraldic bird decoration it bears, attests to the early existence of this form. Discovered in the eighteenth century, this tablet was embellished anew by the Ch'ien-lung emperor whose poem, dated 1786, celebrates the tablet's discovery as a divine token of his own legitimacy.

38. Ma Lin (ca. 1180–after 1256). Hanging scroll: *Portrait of King Yü of the Hsia Dynasty*

39. Jade tablet (*kuei*). Late Neolithic period to early Shang dynasty (second millennium B.C.)

When the Buddha Shakya-muni attained Nirvana, he entrusted the protection of the Law to sixteen disciples, or lohans. In China these Indian holy men came to be revered for their supernatural powers, which enabled them to subdue wild animals and to meditate for extended periods of time—so long that trees would grow up around them. During the twelfth and thirteenth centuries, as the earlier emphasis on the lohans' awe-inspiring attributes gave way to a greater emphasis on their more human nature, lohans were depicted with an almost portraitlike accuracy. In the *Long Scroll of Buddhist Images*, the artist Chang Sheng-wen still follows T'ang (618–907) precedents, picturing the lohans as dwelling in the wilderness. Subinda, for example, is shown deep in meditation, mentally and physically withdrawn from his surroundings in the hollow of a gnarled old tree (pl. 41). By contrast, in the more humanistic interpretation by the Sung court artist Liu Sung-nien, the lohan has been transformed into a learned scholar. Seated before a decorative screen in a contemporary garden setting, he is attended by an acolyte, who approaches with an urgent question concerning a passage of scripture.

40. Liu Sung-nien (active ca. 1175–after 1207). Hanging scroll: *Lohan* (detail)

41. Chang Sheng-wen (active late 12th century). Handscroll: *A Long Scroll of Buddhist Images*, dated 1180 (detail)

42. Chang Sheng-wen (active
late 12th century). Handscroll:
A Long Scroll of Buddhist Images,
dated 1180 (detail)

Chang Sheng-wen's long handscroll illustrating the Buddhist pantheon opens with this colorful imperial procession that shows off the religious, military, and civil elite of the Ta-li kingdom, an autonomous state contemporary with the Sung dynasty located in southwestern China. The high official who leads the procession wears a tall tiaralike hat and voluminous court robe and carries a dragon-headed sword. Behind him stand a monk holding an almsbowl and a small boy, apparently the imperial heir. Behind them stands the emperor, Tuan Chih-hsing (reigned 1172–1200), fourth ruler of Ta-li, wearing a tall

gold crown and a magnificent robe embellished with mountains, clouds, flames, dragons, and other symbols of his power. Chang's scroll, a major commission of the Ta-li court, reveals the importance of this border principality as a melting pot for religious influences emanating from Tibet and western Asia. The region continued to serve as a transfer point for religious doctrines and icons after the defeat of Ta-li and the incorporation of its territory into the Chinese empire by the Mongols.

The Yüan Dynasty: Under Mongol Rule

For the first time in its long history, China, under the Yüan dynasty (1272–1368), was subjugated by foreign conquerors and became part of a larger political entity, the Mongol empire. Ironically, during this century of alien occupation, Chinese culture not only survived but was in fact reinvigorated, and the Mongols, like every other foreign people who had occupied some portion of the Chinese cultural sphere, were unable to govern without recourse to China's own well-established traditions of rulership. The Yüan dynasty thus highlights some of the most durable attributes of Chinese society—its imperial institutions, the dominant role of the educated elite in sustaining cultural continuity, and its potential for renewal.

The first half of the dynasty witnessed a concerted effort on the part of Chinese scholar-officials to educate their Mongol conquerors in the cultural idiom of orthodox Confucian rulership. The effort met with growing success through the 1330s, as Mongol khans in their capital city, Ta-tu (modern Peking), relinquished control over central and western Asian domains and increasingly assumed the role of Chinese emperors. During the 1340s and 1350s, however, internal political cohesion disintegrated as growing factionalism at court, rampant corruption and exploitation, and a succession of natural calamities led to popular uprisings, open rebellion, and finally dynastic collapse.

Khubilai Khan (1215–1294), the first Yüan emperor, continued on the path of world conquest initiated by his grandfather Genghis (died 1215). Proclaimed "Great Khan" in 1260, by 1279 he had vanquished the last claimant to the Sung throne to become the first foreign ruler to subdue all of China, where he presided over the world's largest empire.

The Imperial Painting Academy was discontinued under Khubilai, but artists were regularly employed by his court to produce sculpture, paintings, and decorative arts. Artisans recruited from across the Mongol empire were responsible for introducing into China a number of foreign influences, such as Tibetan Lamaism, a form of Buddhism that, with its emphasis on Tantric magic, appealed to Mongol interests.

In spite of the gradual assimilation of Yüan monarchs, the Mongol conquest imposed a harsh new political reality upon China. Civil service examinations, the traditional means for recruiting talent into the government, were discontinued until 1315, leaving most of China's educated elite disenfranchised. As a group, the literati were largely ignored by the Mongols;

those few who did enter government service often received only minor appointments, either as teachers in local schools or as low-level clerks, while Mongols, Uighurs, western Asians, and other foreign mercenaries and merchants now occupied many of the senior administrative posts within the government. Southern Chinese, having resisted the Mongol invasion the longest, faced a conscious policy of discrimination. Encountering absolutist policies and prejudicial treatment, many scholars living in the south withdrew from government service and lived in humbled circumstances or semiretirement, which afforded them the time and impetus to pursue self-expression through the arts.

One of the greatest cultural contributions of Mongol rule was the reunification of China in 1279 after one and a half centuries of division. Reunification not only brought together two distinct regional cultures, but it also stimulated the revival of earlier Northern Sung traditions long neglected in the south. Drawing on the scholar-official aesthetic of the late Northern Sung, Yüan literati artists explored the possibilities of calligraphic abstraction, replacing forms that were essentially representational with forms that were essentially expressive and self-reflective.

One of the most significant developments in the rise of painting as a vehicle for self-expression was the union of painting, calligraphy, and poetry into a single form of art as Yüan artists began to add inscriptions to their paintings both to elucidate the circumstances surrounding a work's creation and to extend the meaning of the pictorial image. Often a gift to a friend, the work may also bear the inscription of the recipient or a later collector, thus extending its meaning across time as a repository of personal communication between artist and viewer.

Yüan scholar painting is intimate in its nature, created by members of a small coterie of like-minded friends living in the lower Yangtze River delta area of southeastern China. Often they gathered at each other's homes to converse, view works of art, listen to music, paint, and compose poetry. Their places of residence, where these gatherings took place and where the participants sought refuge from the political world, became the subject of innumerable works of art. The scholar's studio, library, and garden became emblems of an alternative world, one defined by the act of withdrawal from public life.

While Yüan scholar-artists explored expressive brush idioms, professional painters continued to work in earlier, inherited traditions. Northern artists perpetuated the monumental landscape tradition of the Northern Sung, while in the south, the academy style was reduced to a vehicle for nostalgia.

In the decorative arts the Mongol conquest brought together diverse regional traditions and introduced new styles from other parts of the greater Mongol empire through trade, migration, and the propagation of religion. Mongol patronage of Tibetan Lamaism and the close association of lamas with the Yüan court were responsible for an influx of artistic styles and religious iconography from Nepal and Tibet. Islamic influences, on the other hand, were introduced through large settlements of Middle Eastern merchants along Central Asian trade routes and in China's port cities, as well as through the massive migration of Muslims into Yunnan Province in southwestern China.

In ceramics the most dramatic artistic innovation of the period was the evolution of blue-and-white porcelain. This new ceramic type, using underglaze cobalt decoration, probably would never have developed without the impetus provided by the Mongols. Under Mongol and Muslim supervision, potters at kiln sites in Ching-te-chen, Kiangsi Province, began experimenting with imported cobalt and producing ceramics for export. The result was a totally new style of ceramic decoration in which large-scale plates and bowls were embellished with densely painted designs that included intricate geometric patterns in the manner of Near Eastern metalwork and lusterware prototypes. Thenceforth, surface decoration, which had been minimal in Sung ceramics, became a prominent element in all the decorative arts.

43. Anonymous (13th century).
Album leaf: *Khubilai Khan as the First
Yüan Emperor, Shih-tsu*

Succumbing to the onslaught of the Mongol hordes and their Chinese allies, the Sung dynasty was extinguished in 1279, and all of China, for the first time in its long history, was occupied by a foreign people. With the fall of the Sung, Khubilai Khan became the ruler of the largest empire the world has ever known. Choosing Peking as the seat of his government, Khubilai made effective use of Chinese administrative techniques in ruling his vast domain, but he was hardly a Chinese ruler. Rather than building a strong central bureaucracy, Khubilai favored the nomadic system of loosely connected administrative units governed by military officials with strong personal loyalties to the throne. The emperor's formal portrait, possibly after one by the Nepalese artist An-ni-ko (1245–1306), presents him as very much a Mongol ruler—dressed in Mongol-style hat and robes. A less formal portrait, by the Chinese court artist Liu Kuan-tao, also reflects Khubilai's adherence to Mongol customs. Here the aging monarch is portrayed in the wintry bleakness of the steppe, hunting with a retinue of non-Chinese retainers, a pastime long eschewed by his Chinese subjects as barbaric. The image may have been intended to reassure Mongol traditionalists at court that their ruler had not lost touch with his nomadic heritage.

44. Liu Kuan-tao (active
ca. 1275–1300). Hanging
scroll: *Khubilai Khan Hunting*,
dated 1280 (detail)

45. Chao Meng-fu
(1254–1322). Handscroll:
*Autumn Colors on the Ch'iao and
Hua Mountains*, dated 1296

Reacting against the overrefined realism favored by the discredited Sung court, Chao Meng-fu led a revolutionary movement that directed art away from naturalistic description toward a new pictorial language based on the same kind of conventionalized brushstrokes used in calligraphy. *Autumn Colors on the Ch'iao and Hua Mountains*, which presents an idyllic scene of farmers and fishermen, is executed with a simple repertoire of ropelike texture strokes and foliage dots to suggest landscape elements, creating a rich tapestry of sensuous textures and abstract rhythms independent of their representational function. Because images of utopia were often set in antiquity, that which was ancient was equated with perfection. Chao's image of a golden age is thus rendered in an archaic, primitive style. Realism is rejected in favor of illogical shifts in scale, stylized trees and reeds, awkward houses, sticklike figures, and schematic mountains, whose forms resemble archaic pictographs.

46. Huang Kung-wang
(1269–1354). Handscroll:
Dwelling in the Fu-ch'un Mountains,
dated 1350 (detail)

Huang Kung-wang's *Dwelling in the Fu-ch'un Mountains*, the most ambitious surviving handscroll composition of the Yüan dynasty, is one of the grandest panoramas in all of Chinese art. At the heart of the painting stands a simple thatched pavilion, where a seated man leans on the railing to contemplate a flock of waterfowl. The prominence of the pavilion and its proximity to two fishermen in skiffs link it to the most famous site in the Fu-ch'un Mountains, the Angling Terrace of the first-century

hermit Yen Tzu-ling. Yen, though a close friend of the emperor, chose to live in obscurity rather than serve in government, thus epitomizing the Taoist ideal of the reclusive life that Huang celebrates in the scroll. Situated at the center of the composition, the pavilion is the symbol of this ideal. It occupies the precise spot in which, according to geomantic principles, the vital energy (ch'i) of the mountain is concentrated; it is embodied in the four dragon pines that spring forth at its base.

首游鴻濛方丈後池上視
玄妙觀方丈後池上視
壁畫竹一枝倣而作因
息齋道人寫其真
于屏上玉立遺墨在焉
憶舊將羊想而成以
示佛奴以廣游目云

47. Wu Chen (1280–1354).
Album leaf from *Manual of Ink-Bamboo*, dated 1350

48. Porcelain incense burner.
Ko ware. Southern Sung to
Yüan dynasty (13th–14th
century)

Bamboo, painted in monochrome, was a favorite subject of
Yüan scholar-artists because of its intimate connection to the
brush methods of calligraphy. Wu Chen drew inspiration from
the Northern Sung master Wen T'ung (pl. 16) in visualizing the
entire bamboo plant before applying his brush to paper, but
ultimately he was more interested in the abstract and compositional possibilities of the genre than in naturalistic representation. Examples of Yüan Ko ware show a similar emphasis on
pattern, making the subtle crackling of the surface more
assertive and emphasizing the abstract potential of line and
ground.

49. Anonymous (14th century).
Handscroll: *Portrait of Ni
Tsan*, ca. 1340 (detail)

In both his art and his life Ni Tsan was the quintessential
scholar-artist. This anonymous portrait made about 1340 shows
him as a wealthy young dilettante seated on a dais and fastidi-
ously dressed in a white linen robe. The antiquities that sur-
round him bespeak an appreciation of the past; his poised
brush and paper indicate an active engagement with poetry and
painting; and the austere monochrome landscape screen
behind him—which resembles his own paintings—reflects a
high-minded detachment from worldly pleasures. In *The Jung-hsi
Studio*, Ni achieves a quality of thinness, transparency, and light-
ness, but without sacrificing the illusion of substantiality and
three-dimensionality. The painting presents a graceful progres-
sion of landscape elements that move from near to far in a sat-
isfying balance of spareness and complexity. The structure of
the composition is based on a rhythmic repetition of diagonals,
the sloping lines of the pavilion roof echoed in the spreading
treetops and receding shorelines. It is precisely this holding of
competing pictorial and compositional components in dynamic
equilibrium that makes the painting a masterpiece.

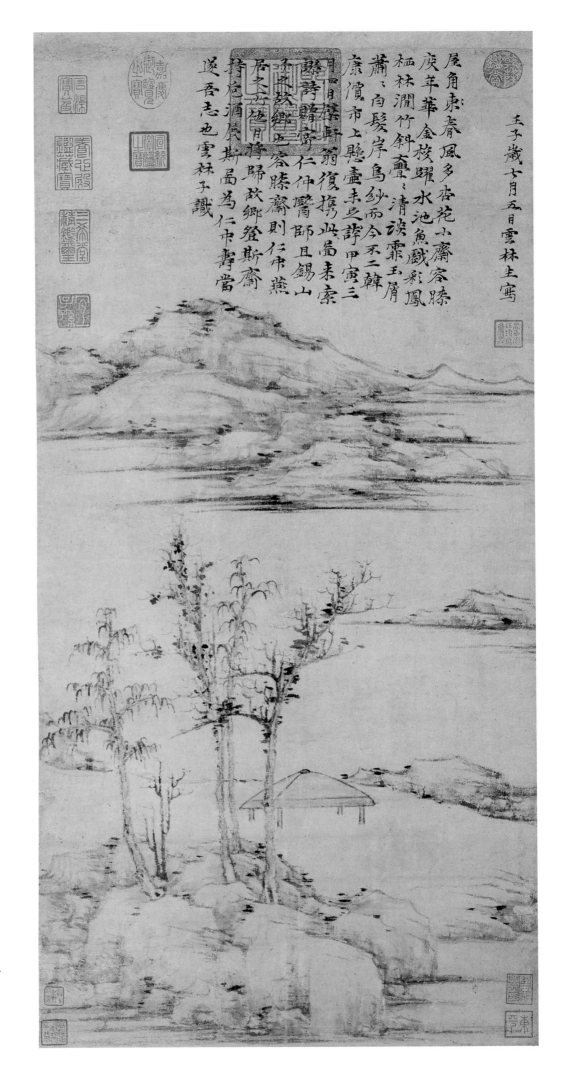

50. Ni Tsan (1306–1374).
Hanging scroll: *The Jung-hsi
Studio*, dated 1372

The *guri* pattern that embellishes this lacquer box derives from the ring-shaped sword pommel. The deeply carved surface, painstakingly composed of alternating black and red layers of lacquer on wood, recalls the eroded forms of rocks found near Lake T'ai. The Yüan painter Wang Meng also drew inspiration from the convoluted forms of these unusual rocks in his painting of the famous grotto at Chü-ch'ü. Indeed, Wang's entire landscape resembles a fantastic garden rockery. Abandoning all suggestion of spatial recession, Wang confronts the viewer with a densely textured wall of rock and water. Buildings and figures of hermits are isolated in pockets of space hollowed from the rock, creating a vision of an enclosed and sequestered environment that lies outside the real world. Reviving the archaic spatial structure of tenth-century paintings, Wang organizes his composition into discrete space cells as a further means of evoking the idyllic simplicity of high antiquity.

51. Lacquer box. Yüan dynasty (1272–1368)

52. Wang Meng
(ca. 1308–1385) Hanging
scroll: *Forest Chamber Grotto at Chü-ch'ü*, after 1368 (detail)

The Ming Dynasty:
Empire of Restoration

The founder of the Ming dynasty (1368–1644), Chu Yüan-chang (1328–1398), having successfully defeated his rivals and expelled the Mongols from China, immediately set about reestablishing imperial institutions, rebuilding the central bureaucracy, and asserting his right as the inheritor of the Mandate of Heaven. The Ming dynasty, thus begun, lasted nearly three hundred years. At its outset, the dynasty witnessed a period of dynamic political and cultural expansion, as early Ming emperors actively directed military campaigns, proclaimed new laws, and managed state affairs. After the death of the Hsüan-te emperor (reigned 1426–35), however, the willful young rulers who succeeded him were increasingly passive and self-absorbed, and the dynasty entered a period of military setback and political decline. During the sixteenth and early seventeenth centuries, although corruption at court led to political disillusionment, a burgeoning urban life and the expanding literati culture provided a stimulus to change and innovation, which was in turn reflected in the diversity of artistic expression.

Economically, China in the sixteenth century underwent a radical transformation through the development of protoindustrial enterprises such as ceramic and textile manufacturing. As prosperity stimulated literacy among the populace, an increasing demand for printed books and works of art, coupled with an upsurge in private patronage of the arts by wealthy officials and merchants, spawned the development of new regional cultural centers. By the 1590s, intrigues at court and widespread poverty in the countryside again led to growing unrest. The Wan-li emperor (reigned 1573–1620) neglected the affairs of state, even refusing for the last twenty-five years of his rule to appear at court audiences or to respond to official communications. And by the 1620s, peasant uprisings had spread across northern China, culminating with the sack of the capital, Peking, by a rebel army in 1644 and the suicide of the last Ming emperor.

In the arts the early Ming dynasty was a period of cultural restoration and expansion. With the defeat of the Mongols and the reestablishment of an indigenous Chinese ruling house came a reassertion of imperial power and the imposition of court-dictated styles in the arts. Painters recruited by the early Ming court were directed to return to didactic and realistic representation, in emulation of the styles of the Sung Imperial Painting Academy. Large-scale landscapes, flower-and-bird compositions, and figural narratives were particularly favored as images that would glorify the new dynasty and convey its benevolence, virtue, and majesty.

Detail, plate 66

An early preference for the Northern Sung monumental landscape idioms was supplanted in the mid-fifteenth century by an abbreviated inkwash manner derived from the Southern Sung masters Ma Yüan and Hsia Kuei. This so-called Ma-Hsia style had survived during the Yüan dynasty as a local tradition in the area around the old Southern Sung capital, Hangchow. In the fifteenth century this regional painting style, later identified as the Che school (after Chekiang Province where it was centered), enjoyed a major revival among Ming court and professional painters.

Ming practitioners of flower-and-bird painting worked in both the Northern Sung tradition of fine ink outlines filled in with brilliant mineral colors and in an idiom of bold monochrome brushwork and graded ink washes first employed by Ch'an (Zen) Buddhist monk-artists during the Southern Sung period. Given the symbolic and decorative functions of most court art, the earlier representational purpose of such images was increasingly overshadowed by an interest in decorative pattern and the conventionalizing of imagery into stock groupings such as the three friends of winter, the flowers of the four seasons, and the four gentlemanly accomplishments. The same repertoire of images appears in the decorative arts of the period.

Early Ming decorative arts inherited the richly eclectic legacy of the Mongol Yüan dynasty, which included both regional Chinese traditions and foreign influences. The varied styles of jade carving during the Yüan and Ming periods, for example, reflect techniques transmitted from the non-Chinese Liao (916–1127) and Chin (1115–1234) dynasties of northern China, as well as from the Southern Sung. The fourteenth-century development of blue-and-white porcelain and cloisonné enamelware, on the other hand, arose in response to lively trade with the Islamic world, and many early Ming blue-and-white ceramics continue to show a strong Middle Eastern influence. The influx of Nepali-Tibetan iconography during the Yüan period was also perpetuated under early Ming rulers, who continued to patronize Tibetan Lamaism. The Yung-lo emperor (reigned 1403–24), in particular, encouraged contacts with foreign countries as a way of projecting his authority beyond China's borders. In 1404 he initiated the first of seven voyages to solicit tribute from Southeast Asian kingdoms, expanding Chinese maritime power as far as India and the eastern coast of Africa.

Although the evolution of early Ming art was influenced by diverse traditions, a special Bureau of Design ensured that a uniform standard of decoration was established for imperial productions in ceramics, textiles, metalwork, and lacquer. The new importance of pictorial imagery within the standard repertoire of Ming motifs—flowers and birds, figural narratives, landscape, architecture, and the ubiquitous imperial dragon—reflects the direct involvement of the Imperial Painting Academy in creating models for the other arts. In ceramics the introduction of color glazes may also be seen as an outgrowth of this more painterly approach to decoration.

The distinction between professional court painters and scholar-amateur artists that had begun in the eleventh century continued into the Ming. While

Ming professional painters followed the representational idiom of the Sung, creating technically polished images that emphasized vivid coloring, intricate brushwork, and bold compositional design, scholar-artists, developing the calligraphic idiom of the Yüan, created works that were more intimate and self-expressive. The literati culture was revived primarily in the Wu region, around Soochow, which by the end of the fifteenth century was the cultural and commercial center of the empire.

By the early sixteenth century, the traditional distinctions between artisan-professional and scholar-amateur had begun to break down. Because the educational system produced thousands more educated men than the bureaucracy could absorb, scholars who were unsuccessful in their pursuit of an official career increasingly became professional artists. In contrast to the scholar-amateurs, who drew inspiration from the Yüan masters, the professionals responded to the demands of a new urban middle class by creating another type of painting, one that drew inspiration from the lyric representations of the Southern Sung Academy. Unlike the monumental wall hangings of the Che school professionals, which are dominated by conventionalized imagery and bold, often bombastic brushwork, the works of the Soochow professional masters are distinguished by a subtle palette and sensitive drawing and achieve a lyrical eloquence and unusual emotional depth.

Ming decorative arts were also transformed by an increase in private trade and the use of mass-production techniques. As imperial patronage declined and hired craftsmen replaced corvée laborers in government workshops, the court had to compete with commercial enterprises for goods and services. Assembly-line production meant that the quality of palace wares in many arts was hardly different from that of the finer commercial products. Decorative styles and imagery were also increasingly influenced by popular taste. In place of the sensitive palette of early Ming ceramics, strong colors were used extensively, not only in porcelain decoration but also in lacquers, color printing, and textiles.

In the diverse, highly commercialized art world of the late Ming, a group of artists from Sung-chiang (near modern-day Shanghai) led by Tung Ch'i-ch'ang (1555–1636), the foremost landscape painter and theorist of the early seventeenth century, pursued a course of artistic reform. Reacting against what he perceived as the decadent and perverse trends of contemporary landscape painting, Tung, following in the literati tradition, sought a creative reconstruction of the past through the critical study of ancient styles. While basing his art on the study of old masters, however, Tung, in an attempt to restore simplicity and vitality to painting, advocated a spiritual correspondence with rather than a literal imitation of early models and underscored the importance of self-expression. Approaching painting as though it were calligraphy, in his landscapes Tung alternated positive and negative patterns, which resulted in a radical kinesthetic style that ironically, during the Ch'ing period, became the basis of the orthodox style in painting.

The fragmentation of the Mongol Yüan dynasty into competing rebel camps culminated in 1368, when one rebel leader, Chu Yüan-chang, succeeded in defeating his rivals, expelling the Mongols from China, and establishing his own Ming dynasty. During his thirty-year reign, Chu set about reestablishing imperial institutions, rebuilding the central bureaucracy, and asserting his place as the inheritor of the Mandate of Heaven. After his death, his fourth son, the Yung-lo emperor—portrayed here— usurped the throne from his nephew and moved the primary capital from Nanking to Peking, where he laid out a vast walled compound and the main halls of an imperial palace. It is known today as the Forbidden City. In this official portrait the emperor is depicted in a manner that, while it provides an accurate description of his physical appearance, endows him with a countenance of majesty and reverence, a requirement for any imperial portrait. The emperor's long beard and curling mustache bear a striking resemblance to those of the dragon on this blue-and-white porcelain vase, which was made during his reign. As the supreme symbol of nature's power, the dragon has long been an emblem of the emperor in China. During the Ming, it became a ubiquitous image in all the arts commissioned by the court.

53. Anonymous (15th century). Hanging scroll: *Portrait of the Yung-lo Emperor*

54. Porcelain vase. Ming dynasty, Yung-lo reign (1403–24)

55. Porcelain flask. Ming
dynasty, Yung-lo reign
(1403–24)

The greatest innovation in Chinese ceramics of the fourteenth century was the production of blue-and-white porcelain. First created during the Mongol Yüan dynasty, when the Chinese actively traded with Central Asia and the Near East, blue-and-white porcelain was probably made in response to the demands of foreign markets. The flat-sided flask derives from an Islamic prototype and is decorated with figures of Central Asian musicians, while a ewer shaped like a Tibetan monk's cap and bearing a Tibetan inscription attests to the continuing influence of the Tibetan Lamaist religion under the Yung-lo emperor and his successors. In an effort to increase China's prestige abroad, Yung-lo initiated seven grand voyages to solicit tribute from Southeast Asian kingdoms. These expeditions, which anticipated European naval exploration by several generations and dwarfed European efforts in scale (each involved more than three hundred ships and nearly 30,000 sailors), projected Chinese maritime power as far as India and the east coast of Africa. They were abruptly halted after Yung-lo's death, but they led to the dispersal of Ming porcelain across Southeast Asia and beyond.

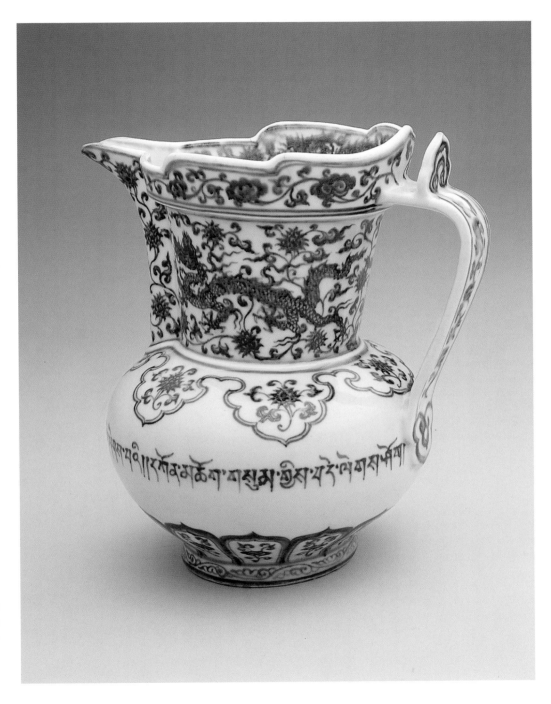

56. Porcelain ewer. Ming dynasty, Hsüan-te reign (1426–35)

57. Lacquer vase. Early Ming
dynasty (14th–early 15th
century)

58. Jade cup. Yüan to early
Ming dynasty (late 13th–14th
century)

The arts of lacquerware and jade carving, which had flourished
under imperial patronage in the Southern Sung period, were
restored to prominence during the early Ming as part of a
court-sponsored revival of the arts. This red lacquer vase, decorated with a dense pattern of floral motifs, bears the incised
mark of the Yung-lo reign but is carved in the Yüan style of
high relief and may well date to the fourteenth rather than the
fifteenth century—a product of the Yüan period appropriated
for use by the Yung-lo emperor. The cup sculpted from
nephrite, a common form of jade that was probably imported
from Khotan in Central Asia, revives the Han-dynasty motif of
the sinuous dragon, whose arched back and head here form the
handle.

59. Jade stand. Yüan dynasty
(1272–1368) or later

60. Shang Hsi (active ca.
second quarter of 15th
century). Hanging scroll:
*Four Immortals Honoring the God
of Longevity*, 1430s (detail)

One of the Mongol court's greatest legacies to Ming China was its
broad support of institutional religion, which extended to various
popular sects of Taoism. Among the most popular Taoist saints
were the Eight Immortals, four of whom were depicted by the
early Ming court painter Shang Hsi on this large hanging scroll. In
this detail, which shows the immortals miraculously crossing the
sea, Li T'ieh-kuai, who was forced to occupy the body of a lame
beggar when his own body was cremated, is shown balancing on
a crutch; his companion, Liu Hai, rides atop a three-legged toad.
Overhead, the god of longevity soars through the sky on a crane.
The jade stand, reflecting the perennial Chinese interest in anchor-
ing contemporary styles on ancient precedents, represents the con-
flation of a Han dynasty lamp made in the form of a ram with the
image of an immortal riding on the back of a fabulous animal. The
Mongol-style hat worn by the figure identifies this as an archaistic
work of the Yüan period.

During the fifteenth century, the Ming court sponsored a full-scale revival of the subject matter and styles favored by the Sung Imperial Painting Academy. The flower-and-bird paintings of Pien Wen-chin, the acknowledged master of that genre during the Ming, are flawlessly executed in fine, precise brushwork and delicately colored in the highly descriptive and naturalistic tradition of the Sung Academy. Only the calligraphic character of the drawing, particularly noticeable in the outline of the leaves, betrays its later date. Paintings of birds and flowers were never viewed as simply decorative images but were intended to convey a moral or didactic message. The elegant garden of Pien's image, for example, with its myriad inhabitants and pine, bamboo, and flowering plum—popular symbols of friendship, integrity, and loyalty—may be read as a well-governed peaceful kingdom. *Pheasant in Snow,* a painting done by the professional artist Lü Chi some fifty years later, presents a solitary pheasant, symbol of gentlemanly virtues, and suggests the proud scholar, who maintains his purity by remaining aloof from society.

61. Pien Wen-chin (ca. 1356–ca. 1428). Hanging scroll: *The Three Friends of Winter and One Hundred Birds,* dated 1413 (detail)

62. Lü Chi (active ca. 1475–ca. 1503). Hanging scroll: *Pheasant in Snow*

63. Sun Lung (active first half
of 15th century). Album leaf
from *Sketches from Life*

The court painter Sun Lung distinguished himself as a master
of the boneless manner of painting, a technique in which ink
and color washes are used without outlines. Working rapidly so
that the colors ran together, Sun created an image imbued with
spontaneity. The same effect is achieved in the elegant little
stem cup decorated with and shaped like a pomegranate. With
its many seeds, the pomegranate is a symbol of fecundity and
an auspicious sign with which to embellish a cup that might
be used to offer wishes for long life and abundant progeny.
With its gentle curves the cup represents a new, more expressive use of clay. The naturalistic colors of the underglaze decoration, a result of unpredictable variations in the reduction of
the copper oxide, reveals the same kind of manipulation of
accidental effects that Sun Lung exploits in his painting.

64. Porcelain stem cup.
Ming dynasty, Hsüan-te reign
(1426–35)

93

65. Porcelain stem cup. Ming
dynasty, Ch'eng-hua reign
(1465–87)

The Southern Sung Academy style epitomized by Ma Yüan (pl. 33) and Hsia Kuei (pl. 35) was rejected at the Ming court by the Yung-lo emperor (reigned 1403–24), who declared it unsuitable because it was no more than the "left-over mountains and stagnant waters" of the dynasty that had lost China to the Mongols. By the 1440s, however, the style had become so popular that it was synonymous with the painting of the Ming Academy. Tai Chin's *Returning Late from a Spring Outing* exemplifies the Ming interpretation of the Southern Sung academic style, with crisp, assured drawing, well-controlled ink washes, and subtle color used to re-create the transitory and lyrical qualities of Ma Yüan and Hsia Kuei. Whereas the Sung artists concentrated on setting land-scape motifs within a plausible three-dimensional space, Tai treats them as flat images art-fully arranged on the picture surface. Ming taste for Sung artistic styles also extended to ceramics. The octagonal cup, although manufactured in the fifteenth century at the imperi-al kiln site of Ching-te-chen in Kiangsi Province, nevertheless bears the celadon color and crackled glaze that are associat-ed with Ko ware, which was produced in thirteenth-century Sung China, in the area around Hangchow (see pl. 48).

66. Tai Chin (1388–1462).
Hanging scroll: *Returning Late
from a Spring Outing*

67. Cloisonné enamel incense burner. Ming dynasty, Hsüan-te reign (1426–35)

68. Anonymous (16th century). Handscroll: *The Imperial Procession to the Ming Mausoleums*, ca. 1550 (detail)

Ritual was a fundamental part of every emperor's life and an essential element in promoting the legitimacy of the dynasty. Whenever the emperor journeyed from the palace, he traveled in a procession, with a vast retinue of state carriages, bodyguards, officials, and hundreds of retainers bearing the ceremonial paraphernalia that embodied his status and power. Indeed, much of the art produced by the court was made to serve the ritual enhancement of the imperial office. *The Imperial Procession to the Ming Mausoleums*, a monumental handscroll more than eighty-five feet long that illustrates the visit of the Chia-ching emperor's (reigned 1522–66) to the Ming imperial tombs some thirty miles north of Peking, is a prime example of the use of painting for documentary and commemorative purposes. Another form of ceremonial art that continued to be created for the court was bronze ritual vessels. But Ming examples, such as this incense burner, were frequently decorated in brilliant cloisonné enamel, a process introduced into China from the West during the Yüan dynasty.

The enjoyment of scholarly pastimes in a garden setting was a common subject in the art of the Ming dynasty. The ornately carved red lacquer box shows two immortals playing chess (*wei-ch'i*) on a pavilion terrace beside a rockery. Tu Chin depicts a similar environment, an elegant garden in which two scholars examine and discuss the attributes of the antique bronzes and ceramics set out before them. Tu Chin became a professional painter after failing his degree examination. Because the number of qualified candidates for civil-service posts greatly exceeded the number of positions available, many scholars became independent agents and sought the support of prosperous merchants living in China's burgeoning urban centers. For these unemployed men of letters the private realm of the garden became the focus of a much-desired alternative lifestyle, as well as a metaphor for an ideal life in retirement.

70. Lacquer box. Ming dynasty, Yung-lo reign (1403–24) or earlier

69. Tu Chin (active ca. 1465–ca. 1509). Hanging scroll: *Enjoying Antiquities* (detail)

71. Shen Chou (1427–1509).
Album leaf from *Drawings from
Life*, dated 1494 (detail)

72. Shen Chou. Album leaf
from *Drawings from Life* (detail)

73. Porcelain cups. Ming
dynasty, Ch'eng-hua reign
(1465–87)

Shen Chou, the patriarch of Ming scholar-artists in Soochow, painted these images at the age of sixty-seven, roguishly observing in his inscription that he sought "to steal the secrets of creation." In the scholarly tradition of calligraphic art, Shen in these sketches attempts to transcend superficial realism, creating a personal interpretation of his subjects through the use of repeating lines, circles, and dots. The resulting images tell us as much about the artist's personality and state of mind as they do about the creatures he depicts. The contemporaneous porcelain cups, decorated in underglaze blue and overglaze enamels with a family of chickens in a garden setting, epitomize the technical perfection that Shen eschews. Executed at one of the official kilns with designs provided by court artists, these thinly potted and delicately painted cups represent the pinnacle of Ming decorated porcelain. Cups like these, highly prized by later collectors, were said to be worth their weight in gold.

為我三彌
納珠占瑞
一閒常会
陶閒常会
恋原自好
小庭士雅
安東三雀
陶畫裏以

101

山靜似太古人情忽澹如
道遠遣世應泉石是
当春雲白媚崖寒風
清菊水霜笙夜不
限我所適丘壑猶
行日無伴微吟嶺
沉同蕭瑟

These paintings present idealized images of two lifestyles pursued by members of the Ming elite. Shen Chou, who spent his life close to home and never pursued an official career, uses the dry brush idiom and spare, refined compositional style of the fourteenth-century scholar-recluse Ni Tsan (pl. 50) to evoke the solitary pleasures of an introspective existence, while his younger contemporary T'ang Yin celebrates the pleasures enjoyed by a scholar-official engaged in a more public life. T'ang took up writing and painting to support himself following his implication in an examination scandal, and gained a reputation as a romantic figure who indulged in reckless living. Here he celebrates an amorous encounter between the tenth-century scholar-official T'ao Ku and the famous courtesan Ch'in Lo-lan. In a secluded corner of an elegant garden, T'ao gazes intently at Ch'in as she strums the p'i-p'a, an instrument of love; a red taper burns suggestively between them, its flame drawn toward the courtesan, as a symbol of erotic love.

74. Shen Chou (1427–1509). Hanging scroll: *Walking with a Staff*, ca. 1485

75. T'ang Yin (1470–1524). Hanging scroll: *T'ao Ku Presents a Poem*, ca. 1515 (detail)

Throughout the sixteenth century, political corruption at court and social and economic upheaval led to a desire for escapist imagery in the arts. One theme particularly favored by wealthy merchants of the time was the Taoist-inspired vision of paradise. In his *Pavilions in the Mountains of the Immortals*, Ch'iu Ying presents a vast complex of palatial pavilions nestled in a mountain valley. Glistening with a magical hallucinatory clarity, the painting is a tour de force of miniature precision and superrealism, technical refinements regarded as signs of divine perfection. Wen Po-jen depicts the legendary isle Fang-hu (Magic Square Jug), which was said to float on the Eastern Sea. His vision of utopia is that of a remote and unattainable domain, separated from the viewer by a vast expanse of water and crowded with archaistic mountains that encircle a palace compound. Stylized cloud scrolls wreath the magic peaks, rising in a blaze of orange vapor and illuminated by a sun of brilliant vermilion.

76. Ch'iu Ying (ca. 1495–1552). Hanging scroll: *Pavilions in the Mountains of the Immortals*, dated 1550 (detail)

77. Wen Po-jen (1502–1575). Hanging scroll: *The Immortals' Isle Fang-hu*, dated 1563

78. Porcelain dish. Ming
dynasty, Wan-li reign
(1573–1620)

79. Ch'iu Ying (ca.
1495–1552). Handscroll:
Spring Morning in the Han Palace,
ca. 1540 (detail)

Ch'iu Ying's *Spring Morning in the Han Palace* was one of the most
celebrated works of the sixteenth century. The original owner, a
wealthy merchant, bought it for the record sum of two hundred taels of silver, more than a year's salary for a court minis-
ter. Compared with palace workshop productions of the time
(see pl. 68), Ch'iu Ying's revival of the ancient subject of daily
palace life is more refined, both in drawing and in use of color.
The painting offers an imaginary tour of the forbidden inner
chambers of the palace, with their genteel pleasures amid luxu-
rious decorative settings, a colorful celebration of the material-
istic lifestyle to which wealthy members of late Ming society
aspired. This detail, which shows an artist painting a portrait of
a lady, may be a self-portrait. The same taste for vivid colors
and extravagant imagery is embodied in the porcelain plate,
which is decorated in "five-color" style with images of the
Taoist gods of good fortune, wealth, and longevity.

80. Ting Yün-p'eng
(1547–ca. 1621). Handscroll:
A Gathering of Lohans, dated
1596 (detail)

In the disintegrating social order that accompanied the final years of the Ming dynasty, messianic religious sects offered the promise of salvation. The peasantry, burdened with heavy taxes and beset with droughts and other natural disasters, were drawn to these often politically subversive movements by their legendary heroes and colorful local deities, among the most popular of whom were the lohans, Buddhist holy men who lived in the mountains to await the coming of the future Buddha. Lohans were believed to possess supernatural powers and are usually depicted with exaggerated exotic features and curious attributes. The lohan Pindala, for example, is always shown with his pet tiger. And indeed, as pictured in Ting Yün-p'eng's painting, Pindala radiates a power and spirituality that might well command the respect of such a beast. In the bamboo-root sculpture of Pindala that was carved one hundred years later, when the empire was enjoying an extended period of prosperity and peace, both lohan and tiger have shed their severe expressions and appear more playful than fierce. More good-luck talismans than objects of religious veneration, these miniature carvings are typical of the intricate workmanship developed in the late Ming and continued into the early Ch'ing.

81. Bamboo lohan. Ch'ing
dynasty (1644–1911)

The late Ming taste for fantasy led to many whimsical creations in the arts. The professional painter Wu Pin was especially fond of creating fantastic or exaggerated images that often have a quality of caricature. In this album Wu has transformed the esoteric incarnations of Buddhist teachings described in the *Surangama Sutra* into accessible, even humorous beings that a lay believer would find appealing. Here the bodhisattva Samathabhadra, who normally sits atop his elephant, is portrayed as the recipient of a gift by his mount, who coyly presents him with two lotus flowers. A similar delight in transforming the ordinary into something startling or strange is apparent in the ewer, used as a container for wine or tea, on which the handle and spout have been cleverly disguised as imaginary creatures crawling across the vessel, itself modeled as a thick handscroll or bundle.

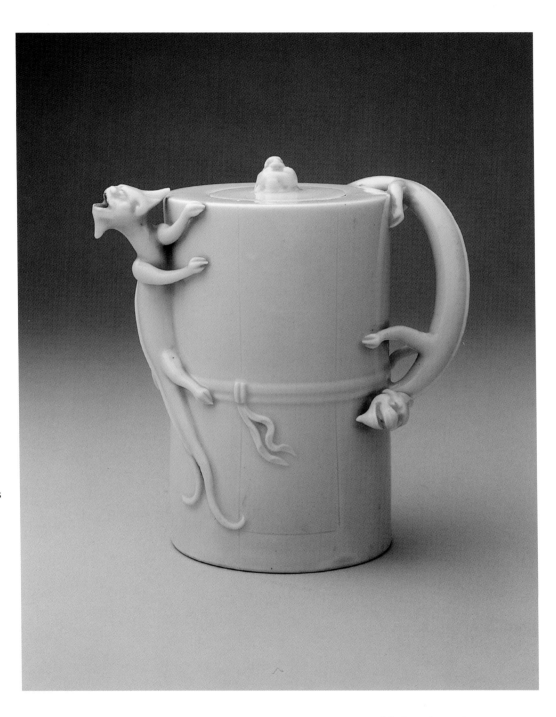

83. Porcelain winepot.
Te-hua ware. Ming dynasty
(early 17th century)

82. Wu Pin (active ca.
1583–1626). Album leaf
from *Twenty-five Buddhist
Deities of the Surangama Sutra*,
late 1610s

One of the four treasures of the scholar's studio—together with inkstones, brushes, and paper—ink cakes molded from fine pine soot or lamp black were ground on a stone moistened with water to produce the medium universally used for Chinese calligraphy and painting. During the late Ming, cakes of ink were fashioned into elegant objects to adorn the writing desk. The Anhwei craftsman Fang Yü-lu even enlisted professional artists to create designs for his inks, which he then promoted through a deluxe edition of woodblock prints. The example of his work shown here is embellished with an image of a celebrated studio rock belonging to the eleventh-century poet Su Shih. Su's rock had reminded him of Mount Ch'ou-ch'ih, a Taoist sacred mountain with a secret passage to a cave-heaven. This same type of ornamental rock undoubtedly inspired Wu Pin's *Steep Ravines and Flying Cascades*, a fantastic re-creation of Northern Sung monumental landscape. Wu's mountain is shaped more by the artist's imagination than by any natural process of erosion. Although the mountain is dotted with realistically described pavilions and bridges, the irrational forms of the powerfully sculpted peaks undermine any sense of natural order and suggest instead an artificial world of fantasy and escape.

84. Wu Pin (active ca. 1583–1626). Hanging scroll: *Steep Ravines and Flying Cascades*, before 1610 (detail)

85. Fang Yü-lu (died ca.
1608). Ink cake. Ming
dynasty (late 16th century)

86. Ch'en Hung-shou
(1598–1652). Album leaf
from Sixteen Views of Living in
Seclusion, dated 1651

87. Jade cup. Southern Sung
to early Ming dynasty
(12th–15th century)

After the fall of the Ming dynasty in 1644, the painter Ch'en Hung-shou, at the age of forty-six, withdrew for a time to a Buddhist monastery to escape political persecution. Disheartened by his failure to come to the aid of the Ming cause, Ch'en eventually resumed his life as a professional painter but became increasingly eccentric in his ways and led a profligate life. In *Sixteen Views of Living in Seclusion*, painted just a few months before he died, the artist casts a nostalgic eye on the pleasures of life in retirement. On this leaf, "Morning Drink," Ch'en alludes to the poet Su Shih, who referred humorously to his habit of drinking wine in the morning as "watering books." Here, the inebriated scholar, languorously relaxing on a bent-root chair, sips from a lotus-leaf-shaped cup with a wine container at his side. Ch'en's inspiration for the drinking cup may well have come from a vessel like this exquisite jade brush washer, which exploits the varied coloring and translucency of the stone to evoke the actual appearance of a lotus leaf. The brush washer may have been made as early as the Southern Sung period, when naturalistic imagery provided inspiration for many decorative art forms.

Bamboo carving as an art form reached its zenith in the seventeenth century in the city of Chia-ting, in an outlying district of modern Shanghai. The brush holder was one of the essential articles used by the scholar in his study. This one bears the signature of the sixteenth-century master Chu San-sung and is carved in low relief with designs by the painter Ch'en Hung-shou (pl. 86) published about 1640 in an illustrated edition of the play *The West Chamber*. The play, one of the best-loved dramas of pre-modern China, tells the story of an impoverished scholar who meets a beautiful lady while she is residing in a lonely monastery. One side of the brush holder shows the lady reading a letter from her lover in front of a screen as her maid peeks from behind it. Reflecting a self-conscious aestheticism then current in the arts, Ch'en has included a picture within a picture, a painting of a bird and flowering branch on the screen—signed by the bamboo carver as if he were signing the painting. The other side shows a garden table with an inkstone, a brush and water-pot, a bronze incense burner, and a lotus in a vase. So detailed is the carving here that one can decipher the crackle pattern on the vase. Another object used by the scholar was the water pot, used to wash brushes. This one was carved to resemble the hollow stump of an ancient pine. The new branch that grows from the right side of the weathered trunk and dips into the hollow suggests the tree's potential for renewal.

88. Bamboo brush holder. Two views. Ming dynasty (mid-17th century)

89. Bamboo water container. Ming dynasty (late 16th–early 17th century)

As tourism throughout China expanded, images of famous sites and scenic landscapes became increasingly popular. *Mount Ch'i-hsia*, by the seventeenth-century Soochow realist Chang Hung, shows a famous Buddhist site near Nanking. Chang's intricately layered details, bathed in luminous color washes, create a richly sensuous quality virtually unmatched by any other work since the Sung period. Tung Ch'i-ch'ang, the leading painter, calligrapher, and critic of the late Ming, rejected realism and instead advocated a subjective style based on the work of fourteenth-century masters. Tung believed that painting should avoid purely imitative representation and be approached like calligraphy. Seeking to animate his compositions with abstract graphic energy, Tung alternately emphasizes the three-dimensional appearance of his rock masses and other landscape motifs and then contradicts that illusion by asserting his brushwork's quality as flat pattern on a two-dimensional surface.

90. Chang Hung (1577– ca. 1652). Hanging scroll: *Mount Ch'i-hsia*, dated 1634 (detail)

91. Tung Ch'i-ch'ang (1555–1636). Hanging scroll: *In the Shade of Summer Trees*, ca. 1635 (detail)

The Ch'ing Dynasty:
A New Orthodoxy

In 1644 the northern Ming capital, Peking, fell to rebel forces, and the Manchus, a nomadic people from the frontier lands of the northeast, seized the opportunity to invade China. The Ch'ing dynasty, established by the Manchus, survived until the founding of the Republic of China in 1911. Combining their native skills as warriors with Chinese techniques of administration, the Manchus gradually softened their early policy of intimidation with a concerted effort at accommodation, winning Chinese allegiance by adopting much of the Ming bureaucratic structure and espousing Confucian ideals of government. But the successful suppression of rebellion and the integration into the society of Ming loyalists was not completed until the K'ang-hsi emperor (reigned 1662–1722) reestablished peace and ushered in an era of reconstruction.

After subduing the Revolt of the Three Feudatories in an eight-year civil war (1673–81), K'ang-hsi initiated a series of inspection tours to the southern centers of commerce and literati culture as a way of consolidating his rule and winning the support of the elite in the Ming loyalist south. An active ruler, K'ang-hsi led armies into Mongolia and made regular hunting expeditions to the Manchu homeland, keeping the Manchu warrior-huntsman tradition alive. He also had strong intellectual interests, was well versed in the Chinese classics, and took an active interest in sponsoring scholarly projects: a dictionary of poetic phrases, a geography of the empire in five hundred chapters, a great compendium on painting and calligraphy, and a massive encyclopedia, the *Synthesis of Books and Illustrations of Ancient and Modern Times*. In 1679 he held a special examination to recruit the best scholars in the land to assist with the compilation of the official *Ming History*.

K'ang-hsi's patronage of these great works of scholarship reflects a broader cultural tradition. Although the Manchu emperors made limited use of Western scientific learning through the employment of Jesuits at court, European technology remained on the periphery of Chinese scholarly concerns, which continued to focus on a critical evaluation of the past and the reappraisal of an ancient heritage.

K'ang-hsi's successor, the Yung-cheng emperor (reigned 1723–35), completed the institutional restructuring of the Ch'ing state, but it was under K'ang-hsi's grandson, the Ch'ien-lung emperor (reigned 1736–95), that the empire reached the height of its power. Through a combination of diplomacy and military force, Ch'ien-lung succeeded in extending his rule

Detail, plate 102

over both China and Central Asia, including Mongolia, Chinese Turkestan, and Tibet. Within China, Ch'ien-lung's strong interest in antiquarianism and research had a tremendous impact on learning. Like his grandfather K'ang-hsi, Ch'ien-lung sponsored many major publications, providing scholarly leadership and employment for thousands of scholars. The largest of these undertakings, a compilation of manuscripts called *The Complete Library of the Four Treasuries*, included full transcriptions or summaries of more than ten thousand works. As many as fifteen thousand copyists were employed on this project for nearly twenty years. This encyclopedic approach to culture also found expression in Ch'ien-lung's assemblage of a vast collection of antiquities and old master paintings that today constitutes China's national patrimony as the collections of the National Palace Museum.

Scholar-artists responded in one of two ways to the Manchu conquest. Ming loyalists, disillusioned by the failure of traditional Confucian values to save the country from corruption and conquest, sought refuge in the anonymity of the Buddhist church or withdrew to the countryside to escape persecution. Working in relative isolation from the traditional centers of culture, they came to be known as the Individualist masters. A second group of scholar-artists sought to preserve the values of traditional culture through a painting style that embodied the principles of the old masters.

The emergence of the Manchu regime as a patron of the arts developed slowly. Artistic production was hardly a priority in the first years of Manchu rule. The imperial workshops had been neglected since the late Ming, and, except for the anonymous artisans who maintained the decoration of the imperial palaces, there was no institutional entity that corresponded to a painting academy. Only in the last decade of the seventeenth century, when the K'ang-hsi emperor commissioned a painting to document his southern inspection tour of 1689, did the arts again rise to prominence in the imperial court. With this commission, based on literati prototypes, the Ch'ing court successfully identified itself with the highest scholarly traditions of Chinese art.

In the plastic arts, as in painting, the Manchus chose to revive established models rather than take a new direction, aspiring to technical perfection rather than innovation. By the 1680s K'ang-hsi had reasserted imperial control over the decorative arts, and official workshops were reestablished both in the capital and in regional centers. The imperial kiln complex was rebuilt at Ching-te-chen, which once again became the center of porcelain production. Early K'ang-hsi porcelains were little more than refined versions of popular wares, but by the end of the K'ang-hsi era potters had expanded their repertoire, reviving monochrome wares and creating a new enamel ware in a pastel palette known as *famille rose*, based on European prototypes.

During the mid-eighteenth century the forms of enamel-decorated wares were usually based on Sung and early Ming examples, and ceramic decoration generally followed antique models, often combining painting, calligraphy, and poetry in the literati manner. But European-style painted decoration also became popular. Using newly invented glazes, potters accentuated the ornate and elaborately detailed. Imitating nonceramic materials and creating trompe-l'oeil effects of metal, stone, and wood, they often came close to negating the primacy of clay and glaze in ceramic art.

Small-scale carvings in stone, wood, bamboo, and such exotic materials as rhinoceros horn and ivory were also produced in great quantities during the mid-eighteenth century. Artisans from craft centers in the south—jade sculptors from Soochow, bamboo carvers from Chia-ting, and ivory carvers from Canton—were recruited by the emperor to produce objects for ritual and daily use and for the ornamentation of palace halls. The art of lacquerware underwent a similar revival: black lacquer inlaid with mother-of-pearl, Japanese-style lacquers decorated with gold and silver, lacquers with brightly painted decoration, and the greatest triumph of Ch'ing lacquer, carved lacquer in cinnabar red.

During his reign Ch'ien-lung sponsored a major revival of court painting to document his accomplishments and military exploits and to promote his image as universal ruler. The new style was characterized by monumental scale, technical finish, and descriptive complexity. The vividly realistic painting style introduced into China by European Jesuit missionaries perfectly suited the emperor's purpose. It is epitomized by the work of the Italian Jesuit painter Giuseppe Castiglione (1688–1766), who arrived in Peking in 1715. Castiglione remained at the Ch'ing court for fifty years, working under the Chinese name Lang Shih-ning and adapting his style to the Chinese taste. Ch'ing academic artists, for their part, adopted Western techniques of linear perspective and chiaroscuro, the modeling of forms by the use of light and shadow. The resulting hybrid style reflects the decorative preference of the emperor and the merging of the artistic traditions of China with those of the West.

浦净渔
舟远
花飞推
路香

93. Porcelain dish. Ch'ing
dynasty, Ch'ien-lung reign
(1736–95)

Wang Hui was the most renowned seventeenth-century interpreter of antique landscape styles. Following his own injunction to "move the mountains of the Sung with the brush idioms of the Yüan," Wang here reduces the descriptive blue-green style of the twelfth century to a dynamic abstract pattern. Combining fine brushwork with a dramatic composition, Wang manages to express emotional intensity in spite of technical precision. Precision is also a dominant element in the blue-and-white decoration of the plate, in which similar landscape motifs are artfully composed to conform to the plate's circular form. The increasing appearance of landscape scenes on porcelain during the seventeenth century demonstrates how widespread scholarly taste, originally the prerogative of the literati elite, had become. Because the painting and firing of the enamels were done in the palace workshops, it is possible that this landscape was actually painted by a court artist.

92. Wang Hui (1632–1717).
Album leaf from *Landscapes and
Flowers*, dated 1672 (detail)

94. Yün Shou-p'ing
(1633–1690). Album leaf
from *Landscapes and Flowers*,
dated 1672 (detail)

Overwhelmed by his friend Wang Hui's genius as a landscapist, Yün Shou-p'ing chose instead to specialize in flower painting and went on to become one of the preeminent masters of that genre. This album leaf is one of six he contributed to a collaborative album the two artists created when they spent several months together in 1672 (see also pl. 92). Brilliantly colored to achieve a heightened realism, Yün's flowers exemplify his revival of the Northern Sung boneless style, in which forms are filled with color washes without the use of ink outlines. In his inscription, Wang Hui praises his friend's achievement, noting that "peonies are difficult to render, because the painting can easily become common and vulgar. In the hands of craftsman-painters, who, without any inspiration, daub on reds and greens, a thousand flowers and a myriad of stamens can look the same." The enamel vase suggests that not all craftsmen lacked painterly imagination. While drawing inspiration from such works as Yün Shou-p'ing's, the delicately shaded peonies may also reflect the influence of European principles of light-and-shade modeling. Probably executed under European supervision in one of the palace workshops, the vase represents a new merging of Chinese and Western techniques and sensibilities.

95. Painted enamel vase. Ch'ing dynasty, K'ang-hsi reign (1662–1722)

The Chinese love of bamboo is made manifest in these two exquisite though utilitarian objects whose forms are inspired by the bamboo plant. The wrist rest, used to support the arm when writing, is carved from bamboo to resemble segments of two parallel stalks. The poetic inscription and leafy branch are carved from the smooth greenish skin of the bamboo, which is left in relief against the darker, fibrous background. A more stylized interpretation of bamboo inspired the form of the porcelain tea caddy, whose body and lid are decorated in bands to suggest a segmented stalk, the leaves growing from the nodes along each joint.

96. Chung-yin pan-shan, Bamboo wrist rest. Ch'ing dynasty (18th century)

97. Porcelain tea caddy. Ch'ing dynasty, K'ang-hsi reign (1662–1722)

乾隆己未春子文小臣黄振效恭製衣

Paintings were often a source of inspiration and provided specific motifs for works in other media. One side of this ivory wrist rest (later mounted as a table screen), which was carved by the noted Cantonese craftsman Huang Chen-hsiao, who was active in the palace workshop during the early Ch'ien-lung era, is decorated with a landscape depicting the famous literary gathering at the Orchid Pavilion at which the fourth-century master Wang Hsi-chih (see pl. 8) created what is perhaps the most famous work of calligraphy in Chinese history. Surprisingly, this precious ivory object was carved to resemble a segment of the common bamboo plant, as indicated by the curved joint along the bottom edge of the screen. The bulging rocks and twisting shape of the mountains are not unlike those in contemporary landscape paintings. Wang Yüanch'i's *Autumn Colors on Mount Hua*, for example, shows a similar cascade of massive boulders, fused together and incorporated into a serpentine compositional movement known as a dragon vein. Carrying one step further Tung Ch'i-ch'ang's (see pl. 91) admonition to animate a painting by the use of dynamic compositional structures, Wang conceives of color as well as brushwork as integral to form, using it to clarify and energize his composition.

98. Huang Chen-hsiao (active early 18th century). Ivory screen. Ch'ing dynasty, Ch'ienlung reign, dated 1739

99. Wang Yüan-ch'i (1642–1715). Hanging scroll: *Autumn Colors on Mount Hua*, dated 1693

One of the most striking features of eighteenth-century Chinese court painting was the influence of European representational techniques. A key figure in establishing the new aesthetic was the Italian Jesuit Giuseppe Castiglione, whose illusionist approach to painting revolutionized court art of the period. Born in Milan, Castiglione arrived in China as a young missionary of twenty-seven and was assigned to work in the palace enameling workshop. Eight years later, after Castiglione was well established at court and had assumed the Chinese name Lang Shih-ning, the Yung-cheng emperor ascended the throne. Multiheaded grains and twin lotuses, believed to be auspicious signs, appeared in fields across the empire, and Castiglione celebrated the event in this painting which he titled *Assembled Blessings*. Although executed in the traditional Chinese media of ink and mineral colors on silk, the painting has a vividly three-dimensional quality, achieved through a subtle use of the Western technique of chiaroscuro, the modeling of forms with light and shadow. This fusion of European and Chinese pictorial methods gave rise to a new, hybrid style. Western engravings and paintings imported into China at this time also provided new motifs for the decorative arts. The porcelain vase shows the eclectic mix that sometimes resulted. The central motif, a Western-style landscape featuring a mother and child, is elaborately framed and set against a French millefleur ground. The handles of the vase are stylized Chinese dragons, but the grisaille decoration encircling the mouth recalls patterns used on porcelains produced in Limoges.

101. Painted porcelain vase. Ch'ing dynasty, Ch'ien-lung reign (1736–95)

100. Giuseppe Castiglione (Lang Shih-ning, 1688–1766). Hanging scroll: *Assembled Blessings*, dated 1723

102. Giuseppe Castiglione,
(Lang Shih-ning, 1688–1766).
Handscroll: *One Hundred Horses*,
dated 1728 (detail)

One Hundred Horses is considered Castiglione's greatest work. A
large handscroll measuring nearly twenty-six feet in length, it
was commissioned in 1723 and completed five years later.
When the Ch'ien-lung emperor viewed the scroll he declared it
a masterpiece and named Castiglione his principal painter. To
execute such a large composition, the artist first made a
preparatory drawing on paper with figures sketched in charcoal
and then precisely rendered in bold ink outlines drawn with a
European pen rather than a Chinese brush. Because painting on
silk does not allow for correction or overpainting, Castiglione
would work out every detail in the final draft before tracing the
design onto the silk. When he began this scroll, Castiglione's
use of Chinese pictorial conventions was still limited. Although
the horses and trees recall Chinese prototypes, the landscape is
still represented in Western-style perspective, with figures
shown in dramatically foreshortened views. The large scale of
the painting also suggests a European influence, as if the artist
had taken a typical Western canvas and extended its length to
make a mural or an architectural frieze.

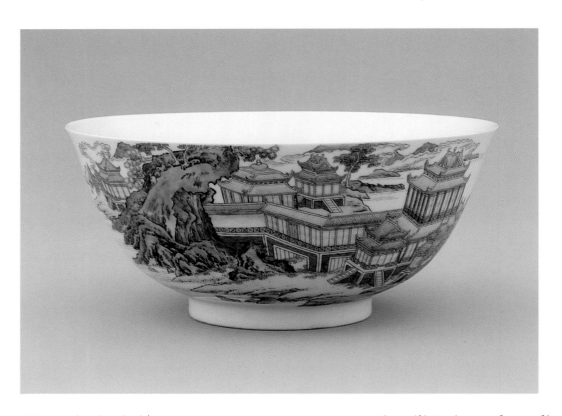

103. Porcelain bowl. Ch'ing dynasty, Ch'ien-lung reign (1736–95)

104. Court artist under the Ch'ien-lung emperor (reigned 1736–95). Hanging scroll: *Activities of the Months: The Twelfth Month*

The *Twelfth Month*, one of a set of hanging scrolls by anonymous court artists illustrating palace life as it unfolds over the months of the year, presents a traditional image of palace halls in a landscape setting but uses the newly perfected Western technique of linear perspective. The picture, which presents an imaginative catalogue of winter activities, including children building a snow lion and sledding on a frozen lake, also reveals the contemporary taste for novelty, as in the fanciful gateway and the European-style two-story structure set among Chinese buildings and courtyards. The fashion of piling up garden rocks to give the impression of a palace emerging from foothills appears both in this painting and in the polychrome decoration on the porcelain bowl, where an enormous rockery is shown encroaching on nearby buildings. This style of garden architecture originated in southeastern China but was transplanted to Peking after the K'ang-hsi and Ch'ien-lung emperors encountered it on their inspection tours to the south.

105. Molded gourd brush
holder. Ch'ing dynasty,
K'ang-hsi reign (1662–1722)

These objects are identified particularly with the K'ang-hsi
emperor, who ruled for sixty years beginning in 1662. The rec-
tangular brush holder is made from a gourd grown in a specially designated area within the Forbidden City. While still on
the vine, the gourd was placed in a mold so that eventually it
took on the desired shape and included the inscriptions on its
four paneled sides. The emperor later presented the brush holder to his favorite grandson, the future Ch'ien-lung emperor,
who encased it in a carved wooden box. The inkstone is made
from a distinctive greenish stone that was especially prized by
the K'ang-hsi emperor because it came from his ancestral
Manchu homeland. Originally fashioned into whetstones,
Sung-hua River stone was first used for inkstones at the emper-
or's suggestion. Taking advantage of the rock's natural colors,
the artist carved it to resemble a melon still attached to its
woody vine. When opened, the top and bottom halves look like
a melon that has been split open; the grinding surface is set
within the hollow heart of the fruit while the inkwell resembles a rough, worm-eaten cavity.

106. Inkstone. Ch'ing
dynasty, K'ang-hsi reign
(1662–1722)

107. Carved wood treasure
box containing 30 items.
Two views. Ch'ing dynasty,
Ch'ien-lung reign (1736–95)

Devices for the presentation and housing of works of art in the Ch'ing imperial collections were art forms in themselves, the most delightful and ingenious being the so-called treasure boxes, which housed small-scale antiquities that replicate in miniature the imperial art collections. Although these specially designed containers may be viewed as a trivialization of art, they are fascinating as microcosms of imperial taste. Ingenuity is evident in the construction of the boxes as well as in the selection of their contents. The four sides of this chest, embellished with landscape paintings after the Four Great Masters of the Yüan (see pls. 46, 47, 50, 52) and calligraphies written in the style of the Four Great Sung Masters (see pls. 17, 18), swing open like folding fans to reveal shelves that display tiny sculptures and miniature antiques. The base also conceals hidden compartments. The large Han-dynasty jade *pi* disk inlaid in the square top of the box reverses the timeless Chinese symbol of the square earth set within the circular cosmos, as if to suggest that the entire universe had been magically reduced to the contents of this one exquisite container. Indeed, in the Ch'ing world view, all that was worth knowing in the universe was encompassed within the

boundaries of the Chinese empire. As the Ch'ien-lung emperor is
said to have remarked to Lord Macartney, emissary from
England's George III: "Our celestial empire possesses all things in
prolific abundance." Unfortunately, the excesses of Ch'ien-lung's
rule—his grandiose palaces and gardens, his costly military campaigns, and his insatiable passion for antiques and works of art—
bankrupted the state and blinded the emperor to the growing
strength of the West. His ultimate legacy, however, is this great
collection, housed in the National Palace Museum, a treasure box
of cultural history.

List of Plates

1. Disk (*pi*). Late Neolithic period to Shang dynasty (2d millennium B.C.). Nephrite, diam. $8\frac{1}{16}$ in. (20.4 cm)

2. Tripod vessel (*ting*), inscribed *Nai sun tso tsu chi ting*. Late Shang dynasty (13th–mid-11th century B.C.). Bronze, h. $32\frac{1}{4}$ in. (81.8 cm), diam. 23 in. (58.3 cm)

3. Wine vessel (the Sung *hu*). Late Western Chou dynasty (mid-9th century–771 B.C.). Bronze, h. $25\frac{1}{8}$ in. (63.9 cm), w. of mouth $8\frac{1}{4}$ in. (21 cm)

4. Pair of pendants (*p'ei*) carved in the shape of dragons. Warring States period (481–221 B.C.). Nephrite, l. $8\frac{1}{8}$ in. (20.5 cm)

5. Standard measure (*liang*). Wang Mang Interregnum (A.D. 9–23), dated A.D. 9. Bronze, diam. of mouth $13\frac{3}{8}$ in. (34 cm), h. $10\frac{1}{16}$ in. (25.6 cm)

6. Chimera (*pi-hsieh*). Han dynasty (206 B.C.–A.D. 220). Nephrite, h. $3\frac{5}{8}$ in (9.3 cm), l. $5\frac{3}{8}$ in. (13.6 cm)

7. Bound marble tablets for the *shan* sacrifices of T'ang emperor Hsüan-tsung (r. 712–56), dated 725. $11\frac{1}{2}$ x $11\frac{3}{4}$ in. (29.2 x 29.8 cm)

8. Early T'ang tracing copy of Wang Hsi-chih (303–361), *Three Passages of Calligraphy: P'ing-an, Ho-ju, and Feng-chü*. Detail. Handscroll, ink on Huang-ying paper, $9\frac{3}{4}$ x $18\frac{3}{8}$ in. (24.7 x 46.8 cm)

9. Huai-su (ca. 735–ca. 799), *Autobiographical Essay*, dated 777. Detail. Handscroll, ink on paper, $11\frac{1}{8}$ x $297\frac{1}{4}$ in. (28.2 x 755 cm)

10. Anonymous (2d half of 10th century), *Portrait of Sung T'ai-tsu*. Hanging scroll, ink and color on silk, $75\frac{1}{4}$ x $66\frac{7}{8}$ in. (191 x 169.7 cm)

11. Anonymous (11th century), *Portrait of Sung Jen-tsung*. Hanging scroll, ink and color on silk, $74\frac{1}{4}$ x $50\frac{3}{4}$ in. (188.5 x 128.8 cm)

12. Fan K'uan (d. after 1023), *Travelers Amid Streams and Mountains*. Hanging scroll, ink and color on silk, $81\frac{1}{4}$ x $40\frac{3}{4}$ in. (206.3 x 103.3 cm)

13. Anonymous (10th–early 11th century), *Deer Among Red Maples*. Detail. Hanging scroll, ink and color on silk, $46\frac{5}{8}$ x $25\frac{3}{8}$ in. (118.5 x 64.6 cm)

14. Ts'ui Po (active ca. 1060–85). *Magpies and Hare*, dated 1061. Hanging scroll, ink and color on silk, $76\frac{1}{2}$ x $40\frac{5}{8}$ in. (193.7 x 103.4 cm)

15. Kuo Hsi (1000–ca. 1090), *Early Spring*, dated 1072. Hanging scroll, ink and color on silk, $62\frac{1}{4}$ x $42\frac{5}{8}$ in. (158.3 x 108.1 cm)

16. Wen T'ung (1018–1079), *Bamboo*, ca. 1070. Hanging scroll, ink on silk, 52 x $41\frac{1}{2}$ in. (132.6 x 105.4 cm)

17. Su Shih (1037–1101), *Poems Written at Huang-chou on the Cold-Food Festival*, datable to 1082. Detail. Handscroll, ink on paper, $13\frac{1}{2}$ x $78\frac{1}{2}$ in. (34 x 119.5 cm)

18. Huang T'ing-chien (1045–1105), colophon, datable to 1100, to Su Shih's *Poems Written at Huang-chou on the Cold-Food Festival*. Detail. Handscroll, ink on paper, $13\frac{1}{2}$ x $78\frac{1}{2}$ in. (34 x 119.5 cm)

19. Dish. Sung to Yüan dynasty (12th–13th century). Porcelain, Chün ware, diam. of mouth $7\frac{3}{8}$ in. (18.8 cm), diam. of foot $4\frac{3}{4}$ in. (12.1 cm), h. $1\frac{1}{8}$ in. (2.9 cm)

20. Emperor Hui-tsung (1082–1135; r. 1101–25), *Two Poems*. Detail. Handscroll, ink on silk, $10\frac{1}{2}$ x $104\frac{1}{8}$ in. (27.2 x 265.9 cm)

21. Oval dish. Northern Sung dynasty (12th century). Porcelain, Ju ware, h. 1 in. (2.7 cm), l. $5\frac{5}{8}$ in. (14.2 cm), w. $3\frac{7}{8}$ in. (9.8 cm)

22. Long-necked bottle. Northern Sung dynasty (960–1127). Porcelain, Ting ware, diam. of mouth $2\frac{7}{8}$ in. (7.2 cm), diam. of base $3\frac{5}{8}$ in. (9.2 cm), h. $6\frac{1}{4}$ in. (15.9 cm)

23. Censer in the shape of a *kuei*. Northern Sung dynasty (960–1127). Porcelain, Ting ware, diam. of mouth $5\frac{1}{4}$ in. (13.4 cm), h. $4\frac{1}{4}$ in. (10.9 cm)

24. Vase (*mei-p'ing*) with incised lotus pattern. Northern Sung dynasty (960–1127). Porcelain, Ting ware, h. 14 in. (35.4 cm)

25. Li T'ang (ca. 1070s–ca. 1150s), *Wind in the Pines Amid Ten Thousand Valleys*, dated 1124. Detail. Hanging scroll, ink and color on silk, $74\frac{1}{8}$ x 55 in. (188.7 x 139.8 cm)

26. *Immortals in a Mountain Pavilion*. Album leaf from *Lou-hui chi-chin ts'e*. Northern Sung dynasty (early 12th century). Tapestry weave, $11\frac{1}{8}$ x $14\frac{1}{8}$ in. (28.2 x 35.8 cm)

27. Bowl in the shape of a lotus. Northern Sung dynasty (12th century). Porcelain, Ju ware, diam. of mouth $6\frac{3}{4}$ in. (16.2 cm), h. $4\frac{1}{16}$ in. (10.4 cm)

28. Attributed to Feng Ta-yu (active mid-12th century), *Lotus Pond*. Fan mounted as an album leaf, ink and color on silk, $9\frac{3}{8}$ x $9\frac{7}{8}$ in. (23.8 x 25.1 cm)

29. Pillow in the shape of a recumbent child. Sung dynasty (960–1279). Porcelain, Ting ware, h. $7\frac{3}{8}$ in. (18.8 cm), l. of base $12\frac{1}{4}$ in. (31 cm), w. of base $5\frac{1}{4}$ in. (13.2 cm)

30. Attributed to Su Han-ch'en (active ca. 1130s–60s), *Winter Play*. Detail. Hanging scroll, ink and color on silk, $77\frac{1}{4}$ x $42\frac{1}{8}$ in. (196.2 x 107.1 cm)

31. Anonymous (12th century), *Hen and Chicks*. Detail. Hanging scroll, ink and color on paper, $16\frac{1}{2}$ x 13 in. (41.9 x 33 cm)

32. Li Ti (active ca. 1163–after 1197), *Kitten*, dated 1174. Album leaf, ink and color on silk, $9\frac{1}{4}$ x $9\frac{1}{2}$ in. (23.6 x 24.1 cm)

33. Ma Yüan (active ca. 1160–after 1225), *Apricot Blossoms*, inscribed by Yang Mei-tzu. Album leaf, ink and color on silk, $9\frac{7}{8}$ x 10 in. (25.8 x 27.3 cm)

34. Mallet-shaped vase with phoenix ears. Southern Sung dynasty (1127–1279). Porcelain, Lung-ch'üan ware, h. 10 in. (25.5 cm), w. $5\frac{7}{8}$ in. (15 cm)

35. Hsia Kuei (active ca. 1200–ca. 1240), *Streams and Mountains, Pure and Remote*. Detail. Handscroll, ink on paper, $18\frac{1}{4}$ x 350 in. (46.5 x 889.1 cm)

36. Gourd-shaped vase. Southern Sung dynasty (1127–1279). Porcelain, Kuan ware, h. $7\frac{3}{8}$ (18.7 cm), w. $3\frac{1}{8}$ in. (8 cm)

37. Ma Lin (ca. 1180–after 1256), *Waiting for Guests by Candlelight*. Fan mounted as an album leaf, ink and color on silk, 9¾ x 10 in. (24.8 x 25.2 cm)

38. Ma Lin (ca. 1180–after 1256), *Portrait of King Yü of the Hsia Dynasty*, from *Confucian Sages and Worthies*. Group of 5 hanging scrolls from an original set of 13, ink and color on silk, 97⅛ x 43⅞ in. (247.8 x 111.3 cm)

39. Tablet (*kuei*) with eagle motif. Late Neolithic period to early Shang dynasty (2d millennium B.C.). Nephrite, l. 12 in. (30.5 cm), w. 2⅞ in. (7.2 cm)

40. Liu Sung-nien (active ca. 1175–after 1207), *Lohan*, from *Images of Lohans*, dated 1207. Group of 3 hanging scrolls from an original set of 16, ink and color on silk, 46⅛ x 22 in. (118.1 x 56 cm)

41,42. Chang Sheng-wen (active late 12th century), *A Long Scroll of Buddhist Images*, inscribed 1180. Detail. Handscroll, ink, colors, and gold on paper, 12 x 635⅛ in. (30.4 x 1881.4 cm)

43. Anonymous (13th century), *Khubilai Khan as the First Yüan Emperor, Shih-tsu*. Album leaf, ink and color on silk, 23⅜ x 18½ in. (59.4 x 47 cm)

44. Liu Kuan-tao (active ca. 1275–1300), *Khubilai Khan Hunting*, dated 1280. Hanging scroll, ink and color on silk, 72 x 41 in. (182.9 x 104.1 cm)

45. Chao Meng-fu (1254–1322), *Autumn Colors on the Ch'iao and Hua Mountains*, dated 1296. Handscroll, ink and color on paper, 11¼ x 36¾ in. (28.4 x 93.2 cm)

46. Huang Kung-wang (1269–1354), *Dwelling in the Fu-ch'un Mountains*, dated 1350. Handscroll, ink on paper, 12⅞ x 251 in. (33 x 636.9 cm)

47. Wu Chen (1280–1354), *Manual of Ink-Bamboo*, dated 1350. Leaf from an album of 20 paintings and 2 leaves of calligraphy, ink on paper, each leaf 16⅞ x 20½ in. (41.3 x 52 cm)

48. Incense burner, Southern Sung to Yüan dynasty (13th–14th century). Porcelain, Ko ware, h. 2⅝ in. (6.8 cm)

49. Anonymous (14th century), *Portrait of Ni Tsan*, ca. 1340. Detail. Handscroll, ink and color on paper, 11⅛ x 24 in. (28.2 x 60.9 cm)

50. Ni Tsan (1306–1374), *The Jung-hsi Studio*, dated 1372. Hanging scroll, ink on paper, 29⅜ x 14 in. (74.7 x 35.5 cm)

51. Round covered box with geometric pattern. Yüan dynasty (1272–1368). Carved black and red lacquer, h. 1¾ in. (4.6 cm), diam. 3½ in. (9 cm)

52. Wang Meng (ca. 1308–1385), *Forest Chamber Grotto at Chü-ch'ü*, after 1368. Detail. Hanging scroll, ink and color on paper, 27⅛ x 16¾ in. (68.7 x 42.5 cm)

53. Anonymous (15th century), *Portrait of the Yung-lo Emperor*. Hanging scroll, ink and color on silk, 86⅝ x 59 in. (220 x 150 cm)

54. Celestial globe vase (*t'ien-ch'iu-p'ing*) with dragon and floral design. Ming dynasty, Yung-lo reign (1403–24). Porcelain painted in underglaze blue, h. 16⅞ in. (42.9 cm), diam. 14⅛ in. (36 cm)

55. Flat-sided flask with scene of musicians in a landscape. Ming dynasty, Yung-lo reign (1403–24). Porcelain with underglaze blue decoration, h. 11¾ (29.7 cm), w. 4¾ in. (12 cm)

56. Monk's-cap ewer with Tibetan inscriptions. Ming dynasty, mark and period of Hsüan-te (r. 1426–35). Porcelain with underglaze blue decoration, h. 8¾ in. (22.2 cm), w. 6¼ in. (16 cm)

57. Vase with floral pattern. Early Ming dynasty (14th–early 15th century), mark of Yung-lo (r. 1403–24). Carved red lacquer, h. 6½ in. (16.6 cm), diam. 4 in. (10 cm)

58. Cup with *chih*-dragon handle. Yüan to early Ming dynasty (late 13th–14th century). Nephrite, diam. 2⅞ in. (7.3 cm)

59. Stand in the shape of a ram with rider. Yüan dynasty (1272–1368) or later. Nephrite, h. 4⅝ in. (11.7 cm)

60. Shang Hsi (active ca. 2d quarter of 15th century), *Four Immortals Honoring the God of Longevity*, 1430s. Detail. Hanging scroll, ink and color on silk, 38¾ x 56⅝ in. (98.3 x 143.8 cm)

61. Pien Wen-chin (ca. 1356–ca. 1428), *The Three Friends of Winter and One Hundred Birds*, dated 1413. Detail. Hanging scroll, ink and color on silk, 59⅝ x 30¾ in. (151.3 x 78.1 cm)

62. Lü Chi (active ca. 1475–ca. 1503), *Pheasant in Snow*. Hanging scroll, ink on paper, 53¼ x 18⅝ in. (135.3 x 47.2 cm)

63. Sun Lung (active 1st half of 15th century), *Sketches from Life*. Leaf from an album of 12 paintings, ink and color on silk, each leaf 9¼ x 8⅝ in. (23.5 x 22 cm)

64. Stem cup with three fruits. Ming dynasty, mark and period of Hsüan-te (r. 1426–35). Porcelain painted in underglaze red; h. 4 in. (10.3 cm), diam. of mouth 4½ in. (11.5 cm)

65. Octagonal stem cup. Ming dynasty, mark and period of Ch'eng-hua (r. 1465–87). Porcelain, imitation Ko ware, h. 3⅝ in. (9.3 cm), diam. of mouth 3¼ in. (8.2 cm)

66. Tai Chin (1388–1462), *Returning Late from a Spring Outing*. Hanging scroll, ink and color on silk, 66⅛ x 32¾ in. (167.9 x 83.1 cm)

67. Incense burner with animal-head ears. Ming dynasty, Hsüan-te (r. 1426–35). Cloisonné enamel, h. 4¾ in. (12 cm), diam. of mouth 4⅜ in. (11.2 cm)

68. Anonymous (16th century), *The Imperial Procession to the Ming Mausoleums*, ca. 1550. Detail. Handscroll, ink and color on silk, 36¼ x 1024⅛ in. (92.1 x 2601.3 cm)

69. Tu Chin (active ca. 1465–ca. 1509), *Enjoying Antiquities*. Detail. Hanging scroll, ink and color on silk, 49⅝ x 73⅝ in. (126.1 x 187 cm)

70. Circular box with garden scene and flowers of the four seasons. Ming dynasty, Yung-lo reign (1403–24) or earlier, mark of Yung-lo. Carved red lacquer, h. 2 in. (5.2 cm), diam. 5⅜ in. (13.6 cm)

71, 72. Shen Chou (1427–1509), *Drawings from Life*, dated 1494. Details of 2 leaves from an album of 16 paintings, ink on paper, each leaf ca. 13¾ x 22⅞ in. (34.7 x 55.4 cm)

73. Pair of chicken cups. Ming dynasty, mark and period of Ch'eng-hua (r. 1465–87). Porcelain with underglaze blue and overglaze enamel decoration (*tou-ts'ai*), h. 1½ in. (3.8 cm), diam. of mouth 3¼ in. (8.3 cm)

74. Shen Chou (1427–1509), *Walking with a Staff*, ca. 1485. Hanging scroll, ink on paper, 62⅝ x 28⅜ in. (159.1 x 72.2 cm)

75. T'ang Yin (1470–1524), *T'ao Ku Presents a Poem*, ca. 1515. Detail. Hanging scroll, ink and color on silk, 66½ x 40¼ in. (168.8 x 102.1 cm)

76. Ch'iu Ying (ca. 1495–1552), *Pavilions in the Mountains of the Immortals*, dated 1550. Detail. Hanging scroll, ink and color on paper, 43½ x 16⅝ in. (110.5 x 42.1 cm)

77. Wen Po-jen (1502–1575), *The Immortals' Isle Fang-hu*, dated 1563. Hanging scroll, ink and color on paper, 47½ x 12½ in. (120.6 x 31.8 cm)

78. Dish with three Taoist immortals. Ming dynasty, mark and period of Wan-li (r. 1573–1620). Porcelain with underglaze blue and overglaze enamel decoration (*wu-ts'ai*), diam. of mouth 8⅛ in. (20.5 cm)

79. Ch'iu Ying (ca. 1495–1552), *Spring Morning in the Han Palace*, ca. 1540. Detail. Handscroll, ink and color on silk, 12 x 226⅜ in. (30.6 x 574.1 cm)

80. Ting Yün-p'eng (1547–ca. 1621), *A Gathering of Lohans*, dated 1596. Detail. Handscroll, ink on paper, 13¼ x 261⅜ in. (33.8 x 663.7 cm)

81. The tiger-taming lohan. Ch'ing dynasty (1644–1911). Carved bamboo, h. 3⅝ in. (9.1 cm)

82. Wu Pin (active ca. 1583–1626), *Twenty-five Buddhist Deities of the Surangama Sutra*, late 1610s. Leaf from an album of 25 paintings, ink and color on silk, each leaf 24½ x 13⅞ in. (62.3 x 35.3 cm)

83. Winepot with *chih*-dragon handle and spout. Ming dynasty (early 17th century). Porcelain, Te-hua ware, h. 6 in. (15.1 cm)

84. Wu Pin (active ca. 1583–1626), formerly attributed to a Sung artist, *Steep Ravines and Flying Cascades*, before 1610. Detail. Hanging scroll, ink on silk, 99½ x 32¼ in. (252.7 x 82.1 cm)

85. Fang Yü-lu (d. ca. 1608), ink cake with Ch'ou-ch'ih rock motif. Ming dynasty (late 16th century). Molded ink, h. ⅞ in. (2.3 cm), diam. 4½ in. (11.3 cm)

86. Ch'en Hung-shou (1598–1652), *Sixteen Views of Living in Seclusion*, dated 1651. Leaf from an album of 16 paintings and 4 leaves of calligraphy, ink and light color on paper, each leaf 8⅜ x 11¾ in. (21.4 x 29.8 cm)

87. Cup in the shape of a lotus leaf. Southern Sung to early Ming dynasty (12th–15th century). Nephrite, l. 6 in. (15.2 cm)

88. Brush holder with a garden scene and figures, signature of Chu San-sung. Two views. Ming dynasty (mid-17th century). Carved bamboo, h. 5⅜ in. (13.5 cm), diam. 3⅜ in. (8.5 cm)

89. Water container with ancient pine. Ming dynasty (late 16th–early 17th century). Carved bamboo, h. 2⅛ in. (5.2 cm), max. l. 5½ in. (14 cm)

90. Chang Hung (1577–ca. 1652), *Mount Ch'i-hsia*, dated 1634. Detail. Hanging scroll, ink and color on paper, 130⅞ x 40⅛ in. (341.9 x 101.8 cm)

91. Tung Ch'i-ch'ang (1555–1636), *In the Shade of Summer Trees*, ca. 1635. Detail. Hanging scroll, ink on paper, 126⅝ x 40¼ in. (321.9 x 102.3 cm)

92. Wang Hui (1632–1717). Detail of an album leaf from *Landscapes and Flowers*, dated 1672. A collaborative album of 12 paintings with Yün Shou-p'ing (1633–1690). Ink and color on paper, each leaf 11¼ x 17 in. (28.5 x 43 cm)

93. Dish with landscape painting. Ch'ing dynasty, mark and period of Ch'ien-lung (r. 1736–95). Porcelain painted in blue and iron-red enamels, diam. 5⅝ in.(14.2 cm)

94. Yün Shou-p'ing (1633–1690). Detail of an album leaf from *Landscapes and Flowers*, dated 1672. A collaborative album of 12 paintings with Wang Hui (1632–1717). Ink and color on paper, each leaf 11¼ x 17 in. (28.5 x 43 cm)

95. Vase with floral decoration. Ch'ing dynasty, mark and period of K'ang-hsi (r. 1662–1722). Painted enamel on copper, h. 5⅜ in. (13.5 cm)

96. Chung-yin pan-shan, Wrist rest in the shape of bamboo sections. Ch'ing dynasty (18th century). Carved bamboo, l. 5⅞ in. (14.8 cm), w. 1¾ in. (4.4 cm)

97. Tea caddy with bamboo leaves. Ch'ing dynasty, mark and period of K'ang-hsi (r. 1662–1722). Porcelain painted in underglaze blue, h. 6¾ in. (17 cm), diam. of base 4½ in. (11.5 cm)

98. Huang Chen-hsiao (active early 18th century), Small screen in the form of a wrist rest with a scene of the Gathering at the Orchid Pavilion. Ch'ing dynasty, dated to fourth year of Ch'ien-lung reign (1739). Carved ivory, h. 3⅝ in. (9.2 cm), w. 1⅝ in. (4 cm)

99. Wang Yüan-ch'i (1642–1715), *Autumn Colors on Mount Hua*, dated 1693. Detail. Hanging scroll, ink and color on paper, 45⅝ x 19⅝ in. (115.9 x 49.7 cm)

100. Giuseppe Castiglione (Lang Shih-ning, 1688–1766), *Assembled Blessings*, dated 1723. Detail. Hanging scroll, ink and color on silk, 68⅛ x 33⅞ in. (173 x 86.1 cm)

101. Vase decorated with European figures in a landscape. Ch'ing dynasty, Ch'ien-lung reign (1736–95). Porcelain painted in polychrome enamels, h. 7½ in. (19.1 cm)

102. Giuseppe Castiglione (Lang Shih-ning, 1688–1766), *One Hundred Horses*, dated 1728. Detail. Handscroll, ink and color on silk, 37¼ x 305⅝ in. (94.5 x 776.2 cm)

103. Bowl with architecture painting. Ch'ing dynasty, mark and period of Ch'ien-lung (r. 1736–95). Porcelain painted in polychrome enamels, h. 2½ in. (6.5 cm), diam. of mouth 5¾ in. (14.5 cm)

104. Court artists under the Ch'ien-lung emperor (r. 1736–95), *Activities of the Months: The Twelfth Month*. Hanging scroll, ink and color on silk, 69¾ x 38 in. (175.8 x 96.7 cm)

105. Brush holder. Ch'ing dynasty, K'ang-hsi reign (1662–1722). Molded gourd, h. 5⅝ in. (14.2 cm)

106. Inkstone carved in the shape of a melon. Ch'ing dynasty, K'ang-hsi reign (1662–1722). Sung-hua River stone, h. 1⅛ in. (3 cm), l. 5¾ in. (14.6 cm), d. 3½ in. (9 cm)

107. Square treasure box containing 30 items. Ch'ing dynasty, Ch'ien-lung reign (1736–95). Carved *tzu-t'an* wood, h. 8¼ in. (21 cm), w. 9⅞ in. (25 cm) x 9⅞ in. (25 cm)